STANDING IN THE FOOTPRINTS OF BEASTS

Standing in the Footprints of Beasts

A MEMOIR-IN-ESSAYS

Danica Klewchuk

Library and Archives Canada Cataloguing in Publication

Title: Standing in the footprints of beasts : essays / Danica Klewchuk.
Names: Klewchuk, Danica, author.
Identifiers: Canadiana (print) 20250165163 | Canadiana (ebook) 20250165201 | ISBN 9781774391228
(softcover) | ISBN 9781774391235 (EPUB)
Subjects: LCSH: Klewchuk, Danica. | LCSH: Klewchuk, Danica — Childhood and youth. | LCSH: Klewchuk,
Danica — Travel. | LCSH: Women — Identity. | CSH: Authors, Canadian (English) — 21st century —
Biography. | LCGFT: Autobiographies. | LCGFT: Essays.
Classification: LCC PS8621.L49 Z46 2025 | DDC C818/.603 — dc23

NeWest Press wishes to acknowledge that the land on which we operate is Treaty 6 territory and Métis Nation of Alberta Region 4, a traditional meeting ground and home for many Indigenous Peoples, including Cree, Saulteaux, Niitsitapi (Blackfoot), Métis, Dene, and Nakota Sioux, since time immemorial.

Editor for the Press: Jennifer Bowering Delisle
Cover design: Sarah Peters, Galley Creative
Interior design: Meredith Thompson (NeWest Press)
Author photo: Nick Purger and Steven Csorba

NeWest Press acknowledges the support of the Canada Council for the Arts, the Government of Alberta through the Ministry of Arts, Culture and Status of Women and the Edmonton Arts Council for support of our publishing program. We acknowledge the financial support of the Government of Canada through the Canada Book Fund for our publishing activities.

NeWest Press
#201, 10131 97 Street
Edmonton, Alberta T5J 0L2
www.newestpress.com

No bison were harmed in the making of this book.
Printed and bound in Canada

1 2 3 4 25 26 27 28

For my mother and Jannie,
without whom this book
would not have been possible

Contents

"You know,

I just don't think

I'm ready for this."

Important Intersection Ahead

When I was young, my father would often take me along on his favorite sort of pilgrimage: to buy the cheapest used vehicle he could find. It didn't matter to him if what was on offer was little more than an enormous, rusted lawn ornament. The hunt was everything to him, an old engine turning over unexpectedly before we took it for a spin across a field, neither of us caring when boulders scraped the body. A slight dent, after all, made little difference.

Among those lazy afternoons I remember most vividly, was the one spent in pursuit of an ancient Chevy pickup truck. Parked in a pasture, with tall grass poking up through the floor, the once-white vehicle was now the colour of a rotted tooth.

While my father and the vehicle's owner went off to discuss the terms of the sale, I was left behind in the cab. Bored, I rifled through the glove compartment and the centre console, finding nothing more interesting than a half-pack of cigarettes. But when I flipped down the visor, a folded copy of *Penthouse* tumbled down into my lap. This was the first time I'd seen pornography. I flipped through with a sort of grotesque fascination, seeing women with yellow mile-high hairdos that resembled hay bales and breasts so large I was sure they were slowly crushing the women beneath them to death.

Would I look like this one day? I wondered, and would it be a bad thing if I didn't? I was not yet ten. I still had a sinewy girl-body and, looking at these women, it seemed unlikely I would ever become anything like them. I glanced up just in time to see my father striding across the field towards me. Envisioning a conversation that I didn't want to have, I frantically stuffed the magazine under my seat.

Of that truck, my father often said you could chuck a cat right through any spot on the fender. In the winter, my brother and I had to don snowsuits just to ride in it. The drafts of Northern Canadian air that came up from the gaps in the floor froze our little legs in icy blasts.

When my mother had to use the truck, she drove slunk down in the driver's seat, attempting not to be seen. I can remember her at the four-way stop near our house, asking me if anyone was coming. My eyes would dart back and forth, overwhelmed by the responsibility. Horns blared all around us as I admitted, "You know, I just don't think I'm ready for this."

The Alberta town where I grew up was overwhelmingly male, thanks to a constant influx of transient oilfield workers. When I was twelve, my father began to make me carry around a length of pipe if I planned to be out after six. I was tall and too skinny—the latter on purpose because it was something I could control. I was too afraid of what my body might become if I fed it. Because of the starvation, my hips failed to round, and my breasts stayed dormant until well into my teens.

I watched my friends as they grew into their bodies, some of them developing those cartoonish proportions I'd so feared. With its bras layered double for support and jeans that suddenly split at the ass, puberty looked like a country I did not wish to visit. I avoided the refrigerator and let the dates on my visa application to that place lapse. But the cloak of childhood was not enough of a deterrent to the local men. They catcalled me regardless of it, as I loped past on foal-like legs, dizzy with hunger.

"Hey girl, you must drink milk, because something's doing your body good," the first of these men shouted from his car window.

Me? I'd thought. *Surely, he's not talking about my body.* Behind me, a car horn sounded, and I came back to myself, skittering the rest of the way across the road as the men laughed.

It was not long after this wake-up call that my father and I took a trip to Saskatchewan, borrowing my mother's more reliable car for the voyage. We drove across the seemingly endless prairie, with its aggressively yellow canola fields and snaking two-lane highways that truncated suddenly following a sign that said, "important intersection ahead." Though there were never any cars coming from any other direction.

It was my job to watch for turnoffs and animals in the road, and to switch the audiobook tapes over. We'd chosen a few that were unsuitable, the quick reveal of incest in V.C. Andrews' *Flowers in the Attic* sending me fumbling for the eject button. Despite those uncomfortable moments, that trip was good for us. We talked and drove and, for once, didn't fight.

Near the end, my father took me shopping. After we'd left the stores and were back on the highway, he posed a question I hadn't expected.

"What are you going to do when you need to start wearing a bra?"

I looked down and saw nothing, so I said nothing.

"You know," he said, "Amazonian women used to cut off one of their breasts so it wouldn't get in the way when they were practicing archery."

"We were supposed to take a left back there," I told him. "Turn around."

At sixteen, I inherited my mother's Toyota Camry. Like so many of our family vehicles, the car was no longer any great beauty. Behind its shabby steering wheel, I turned down logging roads and left the oil pan cover behind. I backed into parking berms, once tearing the muffler clean off. After it was gone, I sometimes found myself idling next to a police car at one of the two sets of stop lights in town. I'd have to coast through the light on fumes, waving like an idiot, as I waited for the cruiser to be far enough in the distance before I hit the gas, a noise like a derby car punching a hole in the quiet of the street.

In the beginning, the car was a carefree thing. My friends and I would pile in and drive to the local Dairy Queen, the only place in town that carried Seattle's free weekly newspaper, *The Stranger*. Over Blizzards, we would read Dan Savage's advice column aloud, tittering at all it contained and offending the nearby tables of blue-hairs. I was trying to gain the sexual knowledge that had been forbidden to me by my brief, but formative, exile in the Christian school system, without having to engage in the actual activities myself.

The Savage Love column covered everything from the basics to why liquid Band-Aid was not a reasonable substitute for condoms. In a couple of years, we'd have cellphones that could tell us these things, but in that moment, we only had each other and those newsprint pages.

I was the last of us to have my first kiss, and sex was not even on the horizon for me. My body was still a stunted thing, shaky after the eating disorder got so bad that I'd stopped being able to ingest solid food for a time. I'd had to make a deal with my doctor to keep him from hospitalizing me. He picked a random number of pounds for me to gain over the next three months, and I'd agreed to it, not bothering to mention how painful I found stepping on a scale to be.

"You'll get the calories from meal-replacement beverages—that's more than you're taking in right now—and you should be able to hold them down," the doctor advised. "Move on to solid food when you can, but beware of anything with seeds and skins for the next while. They're difficult for your body to digest."

My mother stood nearby, intently studying a chart about bone mass, as if it might contain some sort of hidden answer to our current problem. A few days previous, she'd handed me the dog dish from the back of her car, not wanting me to vomit into a Main Street gutter.

While I was dealing with my illness, my girlfriends were coupling in cars parked in church lots during service. They told me which range road to turn down if I wanted to see the flagging cups of their left-behind bras, strung-up on a weathervane by someone's unkind brother. I was scandalized but pretended not to be. I didn't want to seem as green as I was, it made me feel vulnerable. But to my untrained eye, it was starting to seem like there was always a strange man nearby with his dick at the ready. I saw this in the early evenings as I drove past the town mini motel. Tall strangers pissed out front, swinging around to heckle me, with my trembling hands at ten and two on the wheel.

Sometimes, my friends and I took the car for longer trips. Our randy Social Studies teacher would let us skip class and we'd go swimming in the MacLeod River. I remember those days as brilliantly hot, with birds turning slow circles in the sky, their wings backdropped by a flaming sun. The river grew deep quickly, the water at our waists, the current tugging at us. We'd have to link our bodies into human chains to make it back to shore.

On other days, we'd leave the town behind entirely, the smattering of single-storey buildings disappearing into a horizon of gravel roads and oil pumpjacks, the latter's brilliant red heads dipping into the earth like those drinking bird tchotchkes. We'd sometimes come across abandoned houses, the staircases too rickety for us to climb. The walls covered in strange graffiti: sketches of naked women with parabolic breasts and math equations scribbled nearby, as if the two were somehow related.

Sometimes we ventured only as far as the baby graves. On the outskirts of town, down a dirt road and through a path in the trees, was a place you'd have been unable to find unless someone told you about it. Many of the graves featured old wooden crosses with picture frames that now stood empty. Others had only stones, their engravings weathered unreadable. The graves were so much a part of the landscape that I sometimes had to swerve to avoid them, a faded bunch of fabric flowers jutting out of the crusted snow and stopping me in my tracks.

There had been no reason for our visits to that place beyond boredom. It's my hope now that if there are ghosts inhabiting those woods, they are the sort that don't mind company. Though surely, they minded the detritus of our left-behind beer cans.

As teens, we imagined a sinister causality. A series of ritualistic murders. Or maybe a plague that only killed infants. When I was older, I met a young man who was writing his PhD about the gravesite. I learned that the graves mostly belonged to babies because infant mortality rates were so high back then. Also, the tombs weren't really hidden. They were left in the old, abandoned graveyard that was later moved because sandstone slabs a few feet down made digging near impossible. The student shared a particularly memorable anecdote where a gravedigger had cussed his way through an entire memorial service.

As we grew older, our attempts to occupy ourselves grew more desperate. We found a less-than-discerning gas station attendant who'd sell us Roman candles, though we were all underage. We aimed them into old, defunct satellite dishes, hoping that the sparking balls of flame would trace parabolas into them before arcing back towards us. The little fireballs usually landed instead in a distant clump of grass, which would then have to be stamped out.

Occasionally, live shows were held in the tiny music shop on Main Street, with bedsheets tossed over the merchandise. One of the bands, from a nearby rival town, sang about how they were Shelbyville and we were Springfield, the spikes from some punk's jacket leaving welts on the chests of those that got too close.

Out in front of the venue, I, in my greenness, mistook a trail of toothpaste on the sidewalk for semen, as my more experienced friends laughed and laughed. I drove them home listening to the cadence of their guffaws, the one who'd been relegated to riding in the trunk sounding off with muffled giggles that I could still hear over the music.

Looking back now, I see that it was those of us who weren't having sex that embraced the most dangerous outings with gusto. We were unable to distract ourselves with the bodies of others, and so we drank mickies bought for us by older siblings and drove off into whiteouts, the pulled e-brake sending us careening, only to have to dig ourselves out and sober up in the chill of the falling snow.

We were, effectively, nowhere. Close enough to wildlife for our fathers to reason that it was good to keep a gun in the house, even if they (like my own father) only pulled it out to clean it when the new boy we were seeing came over to meet them. There were cougars in the vicinity and dead porcupines left on driver's seats as pranks—the ensuing screams doing much to break up the monotonous silence. For one particularly memorable Valentine's Day, I was given an enormous jar containing a pickled moose heart. My mother insisted I keep it in the garage, and I did so until it froze and then thawed into a cloudy mass.

On the way to school from a friend's place out of town, we drove up the crests of verdant hills as the sun rose, the bright prairie sky a wash of yellow and gold. A slender crescent of the moon remained on the horizon, as if someone had forgotten to put it away. An animal sauntered into the road, completing the idyllic scene. We glanced at it, the car speeding nearer to its flanks.

"Deer," I whispered.

"Oh," my girlfriend said, registering its presence at last. She dropped the razor she'd been using to dry-shave her legs and swerved around the beast, narrowly missing it.

As the years passed, I found my driving routines changed. Soon, I was driving friends to get pregnancy tests and to doctors' appointments. When we went to the river, one of us did so with the rounding belly she was still hiding from her mother at seven months along.

The town, with its transient crush of oilfield workers, grew ever more menacing. They dropped by our teenage parties, leering on the fringes of bonfires as we pretended not to know what they wanted. We never went off to pee by ourselves and even had a name for things that happened to you when you were passed out. We called it being ghost-ridden.

At seventeen, I went out with a man ten years my senior. I was not old enough to go to the bar, and so he bought us milkshakes and asked me about what it was like to grow up here. We drove around afterwards, with him in the passenger's seat. When I dropped him off, he peeled off his shirt to show me the tattoo on his chest, and it occurred to me suddenly how much larger he was than me, and how not ready I was for this moment. I both wanted him and didn't entirely know what this meant. There was a tense pause before he got out, finally striding towards his apartment building, his shirt slung over one shoulder.

I didn't speak to that man again, but he did call for me. Rather than discuss their opposition to my being involved with him, my parents told him I'd moved to live with my grandparents two provinces over. It was a tactic they later admitted to using more than once.

I was at last growing up visibly. The weight I'd agreed to gain had settled on me, and now, though much later than everyone else, I had started to develop. Stretchmarks extended from my nipples to my armpits, making my breasts look like a pair of twin fireworks. I was not ready, but this didn't matter. The men had seen me, and now it was time to leave.

My father paused in his gun cleaning long enough to see that the car I'd been driving wouldn't do to get me away from this town. It smelled of gas in the cab if I idled too long and one of the rear windows had been propped up with blocks of wood. The brakes were nearly gone, too. I had to crest up the last hill into town and flow down the other side without touching the gas so I might be able to stop at the lights a few blocks later.

If the houses on either side of the road flipped by like playing cards, the siding of one blurring into the stucco of another, I'd know I was going too fast. My old horn a smoker's wheeze of warning as I blew through a red.

My father purchased a relatively new car, spending a sum he'd have scoffed at years before, and sent me off into the nearest city with his blessing. I slid into the buttery leather of the gently used driver's seat, my long legs folding in after me. When I pulled down the mirror to block the sun, something fluttered out into my lap. But it was only the former owner's insurance cards, the paper as pink and creased as labial folds.

Standing in the Footprints of Beasts

My parents never particularly liked each other. When I was small, my mother once woke my brother and me in the night and asked, "If I leave your father right now, will you come with me?" Yes, of course. Her love was like a cat's: curious and mercurial. We did not wish to learn what one needed to do to be without it.

My father was the stranger who did shiftwork at the nearby chipboard plant and seemed to materialize in the afternoons, his presence taking us by surprise. As if we'd been caught doing something wrong. Only his anger was familiar to us. Little things would set him off. I often played our conversations over in my head, trying to figure out what had done it this time. In those just-woken moments, he seemed at his most animal-like. His movements were unpredictable as he crossed in front of us, his bare feet sticking audibly with each footfall across the hardwood floor.

My brother and I treated him like an interloper. Once, when I was a toddler, he'd taken us on a trip to Texas to visit his parents in the place where they spent the winter. My mother had agreed to write a letter allowing us to accompany him without her. It was an action she'd agonized over, as she was certain the three of us would never return. I picture that possible future sometimes now, like the plot of an early Emily St. John Mandel novel. My brother and I growing up in the back seats of cars as we sped across the United States, our father at the wheel. My mother is always a few kilometres behind, prowling through the sunburnt grass at rest stops, a hand at her brow visoring her eyes as she squints, furious, into the sun. Enraged, not that we are gone, but that he had dared to take what was not his.

As insurance that she not abscond with us, he'd threatened to tell the courts that she was such an unfit mother she'd be barred from ever seeing us. On nights that our father was at work, we swore our allegiance to our mother. We believed our place was with her, and we'd say whatever we had to. Still, she believed she couldn't risk the scrutiny of a judge. That she might lose.

Neither of them particularly wanted us. My mother reminded us often that she had never wanted her own children. But—and here her words took on a falsely-sunny uptick—she was so glad we were here now. As if we'd had a choice in the matter and had foisted ourselves upon her like long-term guests.

Our parents fought bitterly about who would keep us. My brother and I understood that they were not a true mated pair. I'd read territorial disputes were among the leading causes of death amid wolves, and we wondered when she would decide that this space was exclusively her own, and what that might mean for him, for she was the Luna-wolf.

My brother and I sometimes ran away to sleep under the night sky in the empty field across from our house, frog song and insects singing us to sleep. Our bodies denting the tall grass. My brother woke often on those nights, his fingers seeking me in the stalks, to reassure himself I was still there, that no one had taken me in the night.

Every few hours, the beam of a flashlight would sweep the ground near us. I would shut my eyes tighter against it and the murmuring of one of their voices—never both—my mother or father asking if we were ready to come home now. Then, the sound of footsteps receding back towards the house, without us.

Once, my brother and I made it as far as the United church on the corner. We were four and seven. Our parents came for us in their lumbering motorhome. It crawled along the street beside us until we climbed in, our little legs already tired and our meagre supply of filched granola bars nibbled to nothing. We had been running away from the camping trip that was to follow: rain in the forecast, us shut-up in a small space for days with caged beasts. The two of them stepping out into the downpour to fight, though it made little difference. They kept beneath the camper's awning. And even with the pelting rain, we could hear their every word through the thin fibreglass walls.

God, then, was a surprising blade in their weapons kit. Out of the blue, my father joined a bible study comprised entirely of women. I think now that he was there looking, hoping to find a female more compliant than the one currently stalking the halls of his house. A lamb to his lion. My mother, refusing to be left behind, gained membership to the most riotous church in town. My brother and I followed her, worried she would deviate from the plan and leave us behind one Sunday morning, having taken nothing with her but her best dress and a tasteful pair of pumps. We knew she could do it too, could start again without a thing to her name. We worshipped and feared this about her: that she would flex this muscle just to show us all that it existed there under her skin.

At her church, my brother and I were confronted with a room full of people shrieking gibberish, their bodies quaking and humming as the spirit crashed through their insides like a wild thing. God was the animal we did not anticipate. We had no contingency plan for this and could only stare as a woman at the front began to tremble. Suddenly, she pitched over, her wild black hair flinging out behind her, her face landing squarely on the pillow that waited on the floor. The movement was perfect, as if she did this every Sunday.

My father, always suspicious of our activities without him, began to tag along. And before my mother could refuse, he had signed them up for a church-offered marriage group. After each week's Wednesday session, they would squirrel away to opposite corners of the house to do a better job of the assigned homework than their spouse. Still, it was a slight improvement from the way things had been. After a few weeks, they no longer required my brother and I to pass messages between them.

We were relieved, if a bit suspicious of the ceasefire. How long could it possibly last? We wanted to know, as we lounged on our bellies in the brown shag carpet of my brother's bedroom. His little green army men stood in a line before us, as we tried to plot out the surely encroaching war. Even in those salad days, the church had the whiff of something not quite right.

My first glimpse of something off came from the woman who fell face-first into a pillow at the altar every service. She lived in the little house on the church's property. When invited inside by her daughter, I saw only pale streams of light from the windows that lined one side of the staircase obstructed by trash bags filled with stuff.

Because my brother and I were still our mother's chief confidantes, we learned from her that the falling woman wanted to be compensated for the spiritual warfare she waged on behalf of the congregation and had ceased to pay rent on the house. In response, the church leveled it, quick as the pulverizing hand of a displeased god. One day it was there and the next it was timber. The family that had inhabited it moved into their van in the church parking lot. We'd often see the vehicle, the steaming entrails of its exhaust on a cold winter's day.

"Don't look," my mother would order, as we marched on past. As if looking were dangerous. A glance cast over one shoulder rendering you a pillar of salt.

"They deceived us all, and took from the church," the frothing pastor declared. I risked a glance around the room, my eyes flitting from the thick pile of baby pink carpet to the high white ceilings. It seemed to me the church had more than enough to spare.

I often saw the family at the town library after that, keeping warm in the stacks. The table in front of them piled high with spent paperbacks.

As things shifted within my own home, I began to miss my parents' previous approach towards religion. Before, their actions had been a self-serving enactment of Pascal's Wager. They attended service occasionally, thinking that if God did exist, they'd be covered. If he didn't, well, what was a few hours out of their lives? Back then, there'd been the occasional Lutheran assembly. The pastor was a tall, laid-back man who'd christened my brother and me as infants. You wanted to take communion? Cool. You'd like to take one of the church library books and never give it back? All right then. Or this is what I imagined he'd say to me when I felt guilty about lifting a tiny gold-bound copy of the New Testament.

But now, my mother had found religion and with it that secret heavenly language, all guttural pop and heavy breath. Her chest heaving as if she might puke. She spoke in tongues, as we fought the urge to step away from her. She'd looked sick when under the thrall of Jesus, her body—that thing we'd both dared to crawl from—a point of contagion.

She began to pray over her computer when it got viruses. I watched her from the door of the home office, her flesh greenish and pale in the light. A sea of pop-up ads, the words: *Singles in Your Area* and *Girls! Girls! Girls!* reflected on the shiny skin of her closed eyelids as she interceded for a machine. She began having visions too. At school, I was being bullied, but she assured me there was no reason for concern. She had seen angels in the halls, enormous bright-white beings. They wore basketball shoes that squeaked as they ran up and down the linoleum halls, and though I strained to hear them, I never did. I was dubious of these new skills, certainly. But if anyone had opposed her in them, I'd have gone for their necks. She was, I still believed, all I had in this world.

Though I longed to follow her wherever she went, there was always something making me question the safety of this devotion. I thought of the man in our church who, modelling Jesus in the desert, fasted for a full forty days. I watched as muscle leeched from the shoulders of what had once been a hulking figure, his coats so large it looked as if he'd stolen them from someone with a much larger form. Everyone was so awed by his dedication, but when his skeletal frame bent to hug mine, the staves of his ribs pushing into my chest, I felt only fear for him.

Soon, my parents started teaching the marriage course they had once taken. They dressed in camouflage fatigues every Sunday and blew a shofar, a horn meant to signal a coming war. "God and the Devil are in combat over the sanctity of marriage," my mother insisted, a haze I'd never seen before clouding her doe-brown eyes.

My father, meanwhile, began to soften. His screaming rages came with less frequency, and then not at all. His mounting depression snuffed the fight in him, like a light switching off. Like a house falling. He started to tell me stories of a youth in which he'd broken a wrist while high and walking along some train tracks. He liked motorcycles back then, and his first love had been a female pet beagle named Snoopy. It occurred to me that I'd never really known much about him. Certainly not enough to have given him a chance.

At the church, the claims of the congregation grew increasingly wild. One woman stood before the worshippers telling of how the daughter in the pew beside her had been switched at birth. Luckily, she knew which celebrity was her real child. I wondered not if my mother would follow suit and deny me as her own, but when. I took up old habits: clomping around in her pumps and disappearing into the musk of the clothes in her closet. I sprayed her perfume in the hollows of my body, worried that she would cease to recognize my smell as her own.

When I was fourteen, my parents enrolled me at the local Christian school. It was held inside a tiny Baptist church, with students in the higher grades relegated to portables that sprawled out behind a makeshift basketball court. Everything was tacked on and temporary, the flimsy partitions between classes collapsible as carnival tents.

My homeroom teacher, Mr. R., was a pious man with a spidery gait who had wallpapered the classroom with pictures of the unborn. The fetuses dangled from their umbilici above our heads. In morning science class, Mr. R. talked at length of the sexual dance of bees and the scourge of homosexuality spreading throughout Vancouver and its nearby island.

When my first year at the school ended, I begged my mother to let me return to the public system. Instead, I found myself packed into a classroom at the top of the staircase above the church baptismal tank. The only sources of heat were the radiating bodies of my classmates and the small heat dish we all rushed to sit next to after every break.

In the afternoons, my classmates and I came down from our perch only to be separated by gender. The girls took home economics, while the boys were shuttled to a nearby garage for woodshop. One day, we girls learned that Mr. R. had deviated from the already rather loose curriculum to detail the effects of his recent vasectomy to the boys. Afterwards, I couldn't help but think of him as "fixed," as if he were a neighbourhood stray that could often be found screwing the Pekinese two houses over and something just had to be done about it.

Soon, Mr. R. and his wife began taking my parents' marriage course. He quickly became a fixture in my home, his sock feet sunk deep into the pile of the thick green living room carpet. I tried to keep away and find somewhere, anywhere to go on those nights. But when the northern-Canada temperatures dipped, I often found myself stuck. His presence in that space was an affront to me. He sidled up too close to my body and its new breasts, those soft vulnerable things I hated. I recall only snippets of what we talked about. My classes and interests and what an inspiration my parents were to him and his pale, blade-skinny wife. But I remember, with true clarity, the desperation I felt to get away from him.

So, when I heard gossip about Mr. R. and one of the other students, I felt certain it was true. The girl in question had some cognitive difficulties and, though she was fifteen, she had the reasoning of someone much younger. The rest of us had been explicitly tasked by the school staff with looking out for her. I asked my mother to accompany me to speak with the principal about Mr. R.'s behaviour. The talking to I received was scathing. I was a kid, what did I really know? My mother sat silently, her hands folded demurely in her lap, as the principal lashed out at me alone. This was just talk, and nothing more, she insisted. I was to shut my mouth, and to warn others to do the same.

After I left the Christian School, it came out that Mr. R. had been having sex with the student I'd come to the principal about, and it had gone on for more than a year. The student had put the pieces together during an outreach on sexual purity. It made sense how such a thing could happen. We had been sheltered from learning about our bodies, as if school officials thought not being told something called desire existed would keep us from feeling it and those around us from directing it towards us. They had not accounted for someone like Mr. R. picking up the scent of something he wanted and coming for it while up on his hind legs.

Over those years, I had little bursts of faith, often at Christian youth rallies. These events were filled with beautiful boy-man strangers who looked like gods to me with their golden eyes and lineless skin. We talked about our commitments to wait for marriage, leaning in ever closer to better hear each other speak such private things. There was something about being together with those who had been indoctrinated in the same way I had been. It seemed none of them could hurt me because none knew quite how. There was only the promise of fumbling, of palms over clothing because that was transgression enough for us, our faces reddened and our eyes searching as we asked, *like this?* and *is this okay?* I wanted to press myself against all of them, to discover and be discovered.

At the height of this confusing time, I was dispatched to a Christian summer camp. It was there that I saw holy laughter for the first time. Down the pew from me, a girl I'd met days before bent suddenly in half and stayed that way for some five hours, her body wracked with giggles from the spirit. A handful of us flitted in and out with the things we thought she might need: Kleenex, water, a bucket. The following morning, she couldn't even keep down dry toast. She moaned in pain, a hand hovering over her abdomen, for it was too sensitive to touch. At least, we were told, she had not suffered holy labour. The body trying to birth the spirit. Muscles that we knew nothing about contracting inside our treacherous bodies.

As the week progressed, I watched people form a chain at the front of the sanctuary and fall. Their bodies pitching over backwards under the power of God. Strangers dropped into the arms of men who waited behind to lower them gently to the floor. Curious, I too went to the front and stood waiting for God. But it was only the pastor who came, the wide bands of his striped shirt showing through the lashes of my squinted eyes. He placed his hands on my shoulders, gently at first, then shoving slightly. I stepped forward to catch myself, my foot crushing his.

This is not to say that I didn't believe. I did enough to endure a second baptism in the camp lake, though it had been cordoned off due to a bloom of blue-green algae, the fish all dead and floated-up to the surface, the fetid water rushing up my nose. There were so many of us, our arms crossed over our chests as if in death, the pastor moving on down the line, throwing us one after the other backwards into the murk with a great, tidal splash.

After camp, I went home and threw out all my secular CDs, my copy of Korn's *Follow the Leader* topping the pile, though I would buy it twice more. A friend and pseudo-mother within the church cautioned me on this. "One day, you'll get rid of all the romance novels in your collection because God says you're going to cheat on your husband if you don't. And the next, you'll take it too far and burn everything in your house with hearts on it." She told me of the pyre of things she'd once built in her yard. A blanket knitted with chains of hearts, an old wedding gift, had extinguished the blaze like a sigh of disappointment from the heavens.

Yet as high school ended, the panic set in. I had recently broken up with the only boyfriend I'd ever had, so there would be no quick marriage to hide in. My academic career had been lacklustre, and I was convinced no college would have me. I took a job at a local restaurant and began working six days a week. Most nights I could be found in the dining room after close, covered in condiments, a carafe of someone else's wine in my hand, singing along to a particularly shoddy cover of The Beatles' "Blackbird."

My life took on a routine. I would wake in the afternoons, still in my work uniform, my ratted-up beehive pushed to one side, the pillow shellacked with a thick coating of makeup. As I unwound myself from the bedclothes, I noted the blank spots in my memory. There was never any record of how I'd gotten home. Once free of my blanket cocoon, I'd shower and do it all over again. It was a fragile existence because I was fragile. When one thin gentleman told me I was beautiful; I broke down crying in front of him and his three friends.

At this same time, my parents built a huge, rambling house and began to take in travelling evangelicals. I'd wake up with my usual hangover, only to trot upstairs from my basement bedroom and find an entire Christian dance troupe draped over the kitchen stools. The troupe would gyrate about our kitchen, skidding across the slate floor, while my mother stirred a bowl of pancake batter. This act from her was more disconcerting than the present strangers somehow. In the time it had taken me to grow up my mother had never once done anything so domestic. Now she stood with a flipper in one hand and an apron loosely tied around her waist.

I had liked her more when she broke things for no reason and cursed at the toaster when it caught fire, which happened often. My brother and I sometimes found it jammed full of melted plastic spatulas and blackened wooden spoons, as if she thought the quickest way out of our house was to burn it to the ground.

One morning, the speaker who was staying with us took a particular interest in me. He began name-dropping all the famous people he'd helped bring to Jesus. Included in this list was Head, one of the guitarists from Korn. Behind the seething bloom of a headache I said, "I'll believe in unicorns when I see one."

The speaker demanded an apology, even drawing my parents into the discussion. My mother, perhaps sensing that I was not up to the task of defending myself, shocked us all when she stepped in front of the stranger and suggested he might be more comfortable staying elsewhere.

Still, this altercation reinforced my mother's belief that I needed direction, so I was introduced to a friend of hers from church. Jenny was only a few years older than

I was, but she'd married very young. In the photos of her wedding, she's massively pregnant. In these same photos, her husband, Dave, brandishes a shotgun, as if this old joke is oh so funny. He is smiling, but the look on Jenny's face is more of a grimace: her plum lips a taut, straight line. Now, a half-dozen years into the marriage, Jenny claimed that her kids kept her grounded. But I quickly came to understand that, like my own mother, they just kept her from escaping.

To keep our idle hands busy, Jenny suggested we mentor a peer group of young women on the subject of sexual purity. When we all met up for the first time, the girls were astonished this would be the focus. We quickly found that there was little in the way of scripture to back us up, only the bliss promised to us in marriage as spoken about in Song of Songs, and the threat of men who desired to rape angels but were dissuaded by being offered a man's daughters instead.

Jenny had been raped. She hadn't seen it coming: the way a man could take his power and use it against you. She wanted the girls to be ready for such things. We needed to know how to protect the one thing of value we as women had: our virginity.

On one of those long-lighted northern Canadian days, a handful of us stood in Jenny's yard. Dave taught us that our little fists were no good for punching and how to strike with the heels of our hands instead—something I would reach for years later when a man stepped out of the darkness towards me. Dave taught us that seven pounds of pressure would break a rib, and that if you had to break your finger gouging it into someone's eye-socket so you could get away, well, better that than losing your virtue.

The important thing, Dave said, was to not let anyone get you down onto the ground. It was infinitely harder to fight your way back up once someone's weight was on top of you. He used me to demonstrate, and it all happened fast: the ground shifting beneath my feet, the air rushing from my lungs as my back hit the grass hard, the bulk of Dave's body on top of mine. He coaxed the girls watching to, "See? Do you see how easy it is?" as I tried to draw breath back into me.

Despite such efforts, the group was never overly popular, and after six months with a rotating cast of no more than five members, Jenny and I gave up. Weeks after our final session, I moved away to attend the one college that would have me. Jenny and I stayed in touch, and I visited her whenever I came to town to see my parents.

After a few months passed, I noticed Jenny growing ever more restless. Meanwhile, Dave no longer trusted her to leave the house. I felt his paranoia that she would leave him like a low hum in the air every time I came by. And for a man who owned so many guns that Canadian regulations forced him to register several in Jenny's name, he was hard to ignore. Jenny would talk into the abyss of her coffee while he worked outside. "If we weren't married, I'd date him; I really would. But I'm not ready to be married with two children."

As things steadily worsened between them, Jenny became more focused on catching up on the things she felt her young marriage had forced her to miss. When I came home, we'd go out to Stockyards, the "largest and only" nightclub in town. It was a literal corral where so many hands reached out to grope you from the fray of people that you didn't know whom to blame. The flooring was the same chipboard my father had once helped make at the town mill, now shellacked and sticky with spilled drinks.

I didn't like being there, the waitresses were bruised women with too much eyeliner, most of them shipped in from Fort Mac, a town only slightly worse than our own. I'd hear a song about that place years later, about how you could live and work there, but there was nowhere to stay. Jenny never wanted to leave that bar. The lights would come on, and we'd shuffle out blinking, last call come and gone.

On one such weekend home, I attended a sexual sin conference my mother had buzzed about. She'd helped organize it, and when I waffled about coming, it quickly became clear that I had no choice in the matter. At the conference, I sat near the back with Jenny. We listened to a speaker who'd struck and killed a woman while applying lipstick in her car's vanity mirror. Through this act of manslaughter, the speaker had learned of Jesus from the dead woman's family.

I saw the look of displeasure cross my mother's face as Jenny and I slipped out early. It was still there in my mind's eye as I slid into a booth at a nearby pub: the downturned corners of her mouth and the twitch of her snout as she sensed defiance in the air.

At the pub, two men joined us, one of whom Jenny knew. The stranger took an interest in me. On his cellphone, he flipped through photos of his penis while I kicked Jenny under the table. She drew her legs out of my reach as the stranger switched to photos of his wife, a too-thin woman who was straddling a chair, her lips drawn back to show a snaggle-tooth. "We really love threesomes," he told me.

This was an omen; I see that now.

Jenny necked briefly in the parking lot with the man she'd been talking to, until at last she was ready to leave, cajoling me to come home with her. Even if Dave was angry about her returning so late, he wouldn't yell at her in front of me. He had so many, many guns, I thought as I lifted myself by the holy-shit-handle up into her truck.

By the time we arrived, Dave was already drunk and looking for some company in the hot tub. As soon as we got in, Dave and Jenny started taking turns untying my borrowed bikini top and bottoms. I batted them away, laughing too sharply, a dog bark in the otherwise silent prairie night. I should have left. But it was a long, frigid walk to town on a dirt road that sliced through cougar country.

When we went inside Jenny led me into the shower. She cupped my chin in her hand and asked, "Is this okay?"

I swallowed and said, "Of course." Not understanding what she meant.

We stood under the water in our bathing suits not speaking. Dave wandered in, completely nude. This was the first time I'd seen an adult male naked. His penis bobbed under the spray of the shower, a purple, alien thing. Dave began shampooing Jenny's hair and I left them to it.

I was sitting on the bed in borrowed pajamas waiting for Jenny when they came in. It felt like whatever was going to happen, would happen, whether I said anything or not. They had sex beside me, with Jenny gripping my arm so I couldn't leave. Stray hands floated over my body as I lay there in silence, listening to them breathe, my legs clenched tight together. I did not strike out with my palms. I did not search for eye sockets in the dark. Instead, I froze and waited for it to be over. It could have been worse; I tell myself sometimes now. But that is of little consolation, and worse than what? Why are there tiers to this? Pain is pain.

The lights were off, so, like in that packed bar, I could not tell whose hands were on me, and this made it somehow easier. *So, this is sex,* I remember thinking to myself as their bodies slapped together like so much meat, their chests making a flatulent sound each time they connected. When they ceased to make these noises and their breathing deepened, I went to the bathroom to change back into my clothes. After I found my second sock and the final piece of my outfit, I felt an unfamiliar kind of elation.

As I crept into the kitchen to grab my coat, I saw Jenny seated at the table, waiting for me. "I was going to make pancakes in the morning..." she said sadly.

"Some other time," I lied. Because I knew even then that I never wanted to see her again.

It had snowed during the night and was still coming down lightly. Standing out in the quiet, it felt to me like I was the only person in the world. Before me, there were the thin lines of barbed wire fences capped with snowflakes, snaking perfect chalky lines in the air. I followed the skinny gravel road, stepping off into the ditch as trucks slowed, probably wondering what I was doing all the way out here on foot. When I was halfway to the highway, I came upon a set of large animal footprints that looked fresh. I stood inside them and felt vulnerable and small. I called my brother to come and get me, and, without question, he did.

I ended up missing church the next morning and, much to my mother's disappointment, pretty much every day after that. In the coming weeks, my mother asked me repeatedly what had happened to cause my defection. And finally, I gave her the short version of that night. When I finished, she said only, "Yeah. I thought it was something like that." She had separated from me again, I realized. Left me to guard my own self. And I felt it would always be that way from now on.

"JESUS,

THAT'S A GUN?"

The Roommate Chronicles

Poor in my twenties, I often lived in share houses to save cash. I did not understand that sometimes you can trade sanity for money. The first of these roommates were strangers. I was new to the city and answered the first ad I saw, taking the cheapest room in the place, where only a double bed would fit. On the nights I was really drunk, I could reach out and touch all four walls to stop my world from spinning.

The fourplex I lived in with Twyla and Bess was a concrete monolith among dozens of others just like it that rose out of the desiccated grass like grey teeth in the mouth of a tetracycline baby. When we'd all moved in, there had been talk of renting out the basement. It was an unfinished area with asbestos pipes and warning stickers that said as much. We had no takers of course. The windows weren't up to code, and it seemed like the sort of space you'd need a quick escape from. The only thing I could easily imagine doing downstairs was dying.

In the space, everything came pre-ruined. The carpets were threadbare, the kitchen linoleum curling, the walls already sticky to the touch. Perhaps this was why we were so merciless to it. Shortly after we moved in, it got so bad that if you needed a knife, you'd have to fish it from the slew in the sink, the tip of it stuck painfully between the gaps in your blind, grasping fingers.

My roommates and I mostly avoided each other, except when the couple who shared walls with us could be heard fighting. We'd congregate in the spacious master bedroom, pushing aside dirty plates, old takeout containers, and soiled clothes, to sit together on the bed. Silently, we listened until the man could be heard hitting his partner through the walls. After that, we'd call the police. They would come, an hour or two later, striding to our door and leaning nonchalantly against it, as if they had all the time in the world. The constant sirens heading to the hospital across the street forcing us to yell.

Ours was, admittedly, a terrible neighbourhood. When my mother came to visit for the first time, she reported that the cab driver who dropped her off (a man who'd immigrated to the city after fleeing the war in his home country) had said, "Your daughter really should move."

"It's not as if anyone has been murdered right here," I told my mother, scrounging for some sort of defence.

She looked around at the state of the house in dismay and asked, “How would you even be able to tell?”

On the nights that it stormed outside, the thunder crashing so loud it sounded like the walls might come down, I would sit in the empty bathtub and weep while listening to “New York’s Not My Home” by Jim Croce. I was homesick, not so much for the place that I’d come from, but for the quiet of it. The city was huge and could never fully be known to me. Once upon a time, every back lane and gravel drive had been familiar to me. Now there were main roads and traffic circles and so many, many strangers. I would never know even a fraction of this place, nor where even to begin.

As winter set in, my roommates and I pushed the garbage in the living room to one corner and set up a Christmas tree, a tiny blue spruce that listed to one side. With the trash in the background, the tree looked as if it were travelling through time and had already ended up at a landfill.

“Did it fall off the car on the way here?” I asked Bess, who’d picked it.

“I thought it had character,” she fired back.

My attempts at companionship went from worse to mostly bad, as I traded the guy who slept with not one but two of my friends for another who got punched in the head outside my place by a drunk man who couldn’t find his car. The punched boyfriend ended up in the grass searching for his glasses while I took over for him in the fistfight.

As the months trickled past, my roommates and I got to know the neighbourhood cats by their missing tails and limbs. But even as we were finally settling in, it became clear something wasn't right with the apartment. I developed a case of bronchitis that stayed for eight months. I was forced to cut back on my smoking and, finally, to quit.

When Twyla and I decided that we were going to break the lease, I packed up my dirty clothes and rusted-out knives as quickly as I could. As soon as I left, the pervasive cough dissipated. I tried to put it all behind me, but Bess kept calling. She wanted me to pay out the lease, in full. I gave up on ever seeing my damage deposit again.

I found a room for rent in a house near the city's downtown. The house was old enough to be declared a heritage building but had been festooned with too many additions to qualify. They bubbled out of every side like boils. The roof was bowed like a down-turned mouth, and the lawn so overgrown that the landlord cheerfully warned me that people often threw their garbage on it, thinking the structure was soon to be torn down.

I took a friend with me for the viewing. "I would never live there," she declared after we left, "but I can tell you're going to move in anyway."

"What other choice do I have?" I asked.

"The other place we saw was nice," she offered, referring to a duplex we'd visited earlier in the day.

The woman who owned that place had a brother in jail for murder. He'd escaped once before, and if it happened again, the woman made it clear that I'd have to vacate immediately. It was, after all, his room that I'd be taking.

"Do you even like me?" I asked my friend.

"Sometimes," she said, lighting a cigarette and blowing the smoke in my face. "It really depends on the day."

I moved into the ugly house a few weeks later. My room was in the attic, with a lone window that opened out onto the roof. I thought of it as a sort of patio, and spent my evenings brooding and smoking out there, as I'd taken up the habit again after my bronchitis cleared up.

The landlord was a hoarder, and she used the house as a storage facility. The front room, with its tall stained-glass windows, could have been the most majestic in the house. Instead, it was a rubble of fabric bolts and Japanese screens the landlord made. Most of these were crafted from woven sheet metal and if touched, would cut the shit out of you.

There was also the issue of the gas-powered dryer. When it caught fire, as it sometimes did, we'd just wait it out, too scared to get much closer. All our clothes coming out smelling like ash. A few days after the final, and most spectacular dryer fire, it was replaced with a leaky replica of the same ancient model. Now, when your laundry finished, it didn't smell like you'd been helping to put out a brushfire, but rather, that you'd been the one to start it.

Living in the house with me was Rosa, a drama student with whom I shared the upstairs; Felix and Jude, the two gentlemen who lived in the basement; and Sven, a guy who lived on the main floor.

I didn't meet Sven for the first three months, and when I finally ran across a tall stranger in the kitchen, rifling through the drawers, I had to ask, "Do you live here, or are you just looking for something to steal?"

He glanced around the room. Felix was learning Chinese at the time, and there were little sticky notes with characters on them scattered throughout the room. He'd translated some of them for me: broken toaster, mouldy sandwich, stain.

"What would I steal?" the tall stranger asked me.

"I don't know," I said, "I'll have to get back to you on that."

He grinned at my response and fired a carton of Chinese food into the microwave. This blew the breaker, sending the kitchen into dusk. The oil stains on the popcorn ceiling above us glittered like stars.

"Did you do that on purpose?" I asked, now a little scared.

"Not a chance," he assured me, and began shoveling cold noodles into his mouth.

I started to spend more time with Rosa. She was mercurial, and it was only later we learned this was because she was taking her antidepressants sporadically. She'd sweep down the spiral staircase in a second-hand gown, practicing her drama exercises and convincing me to play along. The two of us would wander through the sitting room with our eyes closed, touching vases and the television, as Rosa grew increasingly annoyed with me.

"Tell me what the window frame feels like," she'd prompt, the lead paint flaking off under my sweeping fingertips like snow.

"Like a bad sunburn," I ventured.

"No, really," she'd say, exasperated, "you're not even trying."

The next day, she'd be unreachable, laid-out on the floor between our rooms. The first time it happened I brought her tea and tried to coax her out of it.

"Do you want me to call someone?" I asked.

"Leave me alone."

"I mean, I'd like to, but I can't get to the washroom."

She moaned and rolled over, so her face was turned away from me. And eventually, though I felt bad about it, I had to step gingerly over her prone body.

Felix and Jude (the guys in the basement) pretty much kept to themselves. Or they did until the pests began to take over. There were mousetraps all over the house, and we rarely checked them. This led to sometimes gruesome discoveries. Once, a mouse turned up under the stove, mashed to a paste, with its tail mysteriously missing. The mice were active, and sometimes you could hear them in the walls, scrabbling about like long-toenailed ghosts. It was the worst when someone boiled water and made toast at the same time, plunging the whole house into darkness. The mice, those bold spectres, would shoot across the floor.

One evening, I heard a high-pitched scream while out on my makeshift patio. I sat, trying to decide if I should call the police, and how long they might take to show up in this, a slightly better neighbourhood than the last I'd lived in.

"That was just me," Jude blurted as he scrambled out onto the roof. "I need you to deal with the mouse I just found in my wastepaper basket."

"Why me?"

"Because you're more of a man than I am."

"...thanks?" I balked.

For protection, Jude taped a flimsy set of oven mitts over my hands. In the basement, I stepped over his pornography collection, gathered up the mouse, trash can and all, and fled with it out into the night.

"Don't tell me if you kill it," Jude cried before I shut the door.

"I'm a vegetarian," I reminded him, as if it mattered.

In the dumpster behind an over-priced flower shop, I poured the mouse into a pile of dead chrysanthemums.

"Sorry," I said into the bin, as the mouse landed with a squeak.

Not long after that night, Felix got crabs for the third time. "I've been through this before," he said, his voice rich with an authoritarian timbre, "so, it's probably best that we all avoid the communal furniture for a while."

"Fuck!" exclaimed Rosa, as she leapt up from the living room couch and sent something beneath it skittering.

We started to circle around the rooms, standing near the furniture, but never getting too close. In the kitchen, a ladybug infestation revealed itself, their speckled bodies climbing the apple-green walls in showy rivers of colour.

I reminded myself repeatedly that ladybugs were lucky, though the left-behind splatters of their urine were probably less so.

I spent more time on the roof, the shingles now dew-slicked in the evenings. When I peered into my little room, it no longer looked so romantic. As I packed, spring set-in, and with it, a drizzly sort of weather. I remembered what the landlord said about the person before me having owned a pet ferret. I realized I could smell it, the scent of rodent piss rising from the swelling floorboards in tandem with the falling rain.

I moved in with a girl named Doris who lived close to the pub where she and I worked. I paid a full damage deposit, though I'm not sure why. I need've only looked around to see that I wouldn't be getting it back. The girl who'd lived in my room had thrown a mulled wine party on the white carpet before moving out.

I settled in, but never did fully unpack. There was no reason to. Doris had too much of everything. Our cupboards contained mismatched towers of glasses stamped with the names of liquor companies, and so much cutlery that the drawer had to be hefted out carefully or you risked having the thing fall and break both your feet. It took me a while to realize why the plates looked so familiar: it was because Doris was stealing them from work.

When she left the bar before I did at the end of the night, I could hear her exit, the things clattering against each other inside the confines of her huge purse. "See you at home," she'd remark, as she flung the strap of her bag over her shoulder too fast. The faint, tinkling sound of breaking glass coming from inside.

Over the months we lived together, we acquired a dozen saltshakers, a pantry full of jumbo-sized canned food, and so much bar citrus that our apartment smelled like an orange grove. If Doris could've figured out how to steal the liquor without getting caught, she'd have cleaned out the backbar too. I pretended this was Doris' way of sticking it to the man—a man who could never remember my name when he came by, though we'd met several times.

It wasn't long before things began to get out of hand. One night, I watched as Doris swept almost every steak knife in the pub into her apron, the black handles bobbing against her belly as she sauntered off.

"Whatever you do," I advised, "don't slip."

She left only two knives behind, so anytime someone ordered a steak I'd find myself in the pub kitchen, ignoring a chicken breast defrosting in a bucket of soaking pasta, and searching desperately for one of the knives.

At night, while Doris and I munched on giant jars of toxic-looking maraschino cherries and quaffed drinks from familiar, frothy pint glasses, I wondered how someone might go about bringing all the stuff back. But then, what if I got caught? How to convince my boss that I was pulling the stack of forks out of my top and not putting them in?

You could see winter settling in just by the things Doris began taking from work: hot chocolate packets, cans of soup, and dozens of perfect white teacups. To avoid the approaching cold front, Doris and her boyfriend decided to embark on a months-long trip to a tropical country. She and I agreed to give up our place, and we began to pack. In the final hours of our lapsing lease, I found myself scouring the apartment alone. I could come up with no better solution for the excess stuff than to fire it onto the loading dock behind the closest Goodwill, long after it had closed for the night.

I started receiving calls from the landlord, though I don't know how she ever got my number. I hadn't been on the original lease. Doris, meanwhile, had disconnected her phone.

"We'll be taking the both of you to court," the woman on the other end of the line shrieked. "I mean…what did you even do to the carpets? They're still soaked."

"Who is this?" I asked, and before she could tell me her name again, I hung up.

By then, I'd gotten wind of a girl in one of my classes who was looking for a roommate. Jamie was renting a two-bedroom basement suite and wanted someone to take over the second room. After frying her laptop by spilling a beer on it, Jamie had entered a wet T-shirt contest for the money and won. Soon after that, she became an exotic dancer, and our shared suite reflected this. Jamie's face was on every page of the calendar in the bathroom. Borrow a pen and bet that there was a little roll-out picture in the cap of my roommate, nude. My favorite item was the old-style steel lunchbox, on it she was topless and bent-over, gardening and courting the worst sunburn of her life.

Everywhere I looked, there was Jamie's face or, at the very least, her ass. When either of our parents came by, Jamie and I would do a sweep of the apartment, taking everything down and tossing it into a closet. Invariably, we'd miss something. I had to stand in front of the fridge for the duration of one of my father's visits, a magnet with Jamie on it hidden behind me, her hands spreading her butt-cheeks apart, a Gerbera daisy placed artfully over her asshole.

Along with all of Jamie's stripper swag, there were stacks of gear for her trade. She had costumes and high-heels and frothy lingerie spilling out of closets. If you opened a door to look for something, you could expect to be brained with a shower of shoes. The worst of these were platforms made of a heavy, clear plastic, filled with cloudy water, inside which a pair of long-dead goldfish bobbed.

I could borrow whatever I liked. That Halloween, I wore her police officer costume, which had a cropped button-up shirt, and ended up doing shots with a bunch of off-duty cops. I walked home afterward, too drunk to figure out the appropriate buses, and woke up with frost-nip around my navel.

"Did you even think to wear a coat?" Jamie scolded me.

"I mean, I definitely thought about it."

"Even strippers wear coats."

"That should be the title of your memoir."

"Oh, fuck off."

She got the last laugh a few days later when I was using her concealer. It was crazily thick, too thick to successfully blend. As I fought with it, Jamie leaned in and whispered, "That, my dear, is for my ass."

It might've all been bliss—Jamie and I got along well—had it not been for the other residents sharing our suite. Jamie was like Noah. She enjoyed having things in pairs. She had not just one tarantula and one python, but two of each. She'd intended to make the snakes part of her act, but they were never quite tame enough.

"You saw that scene from *Blade Runner* and thought it was a good idea, didn't you?" I asked.

"Maybe," she replied.

The snakes sometimes escaped, only to turn up under the fridge, where it was warm. You'd reach into the fridge for cream for your morning coffee, and something would slither over your bare foot. One day I came home from class and found Jamie defrosting mice for her snakes in one of my dead grandmother's antique bowls.

"Do you want to feed them?" she asked, gesticulating at me with the pair of kitchen tongs she was using for the task.

"Nah," I said, scuttling by her, "I'm good."

We started brewing our own wine and beer. Jamie would wander about, flitting between the carboys, her two tarantulas perched atop her breasts like the oddest of pasties. I steered clear of the larger spider, Delia. The one time I'd ventured to stroke her, she'd reared back, firing off little hairs that stuck in my hands like the finest slivers. I often worried Jamie would drop one of the spiders into the brew, and we'd bottle the thing, an eight-legged shiraz aging in the kitchen. Though it couldn't have affected the flavour too much. We were often too drunk by the time we started brewing, and our beer would come out flat and sour. The wine I'm not sure about, as I never tasted it. But I'm getting ahead of myself.

Jamie insisted on having a revolving cast of strange men coming in and out of the suite. She'd call one of them, and I'd stumble into the kitchen the next morning to find a stranger there. Once, it was a long-haired young man, drinking from my carton of almond milk, and wearing only his boxer shorts. He paused mid-sip and wiped his mouth. "I think this milk's gone off," he said, as one of the snakes slithered past his heels. I stood across from him, trying to guess whether he belonged there, or if he was just trying to rob us of breakfast.

Soon, Jamie took up with one of the guys who lived on the main floor of the house. Their place was so full of cocaine and chaos that we'd dubbed it "The Powder Keg" and had mostly kept our distance. But suddenly our door was open to them all the time. Our floor was dusted with a fine power the snakes had trouble gaining purchase in. A couple of months into this new routine, the boys from upstairs had a party. One of them picked a fight with a stranger and ended up tussling in the street in front of our house.

From one of our small windows, Jamie and I watched a car strike the brawling men. The one from our house ended up with a broken femur. I've never been able to forget the noise it made when the vehicle hit, the impact of metal against meat. But when reporters rang our doorbell, we denied knowing a thing.

"I think it's time to close the door between our apartments," Jamie declared.

"Yes please," I muttered.

"And I should probably bring this inside."

From behind the shared washing machine, she fished out a rifle in its case.

"Jesus, that's a gun?"

"What did you think it was?"

"I don't know. A putter?"

Jamie moved on. But I had to fetch her one night, quite drunk, from a date gone awry. Though we both hated the guy, Jamie kept seeing him, and when she got pregnant, they decided to move in together somewhere else. I was away when she left and returned to the suite to find my mattress and all our homebrewed wine gone. In their place, was one of Jamie's snakes.

The house, without Jamie, felt sad. There were only a few windows in the suite, and the lack of light left me feeling like a nightshade vegetable, growing down there in the dark. Months passed. The basement suite flooded twice, filling the laundry room (still full of Jamie's stripper gear) with sewage. I called to see if she wanted her things, but she said that that life was over for her. She couldn't imagine ever dancing again.

My then-boyfriend and I moved into a one-bedroom apartment downtown together, though our relationship didn't last. I soon found myself alone. I thought about renting out the living room and sharing my space with yet another stranger. But I could afford not to and decided that it might be time to learn to live by myself.

The apartment was nothing special, and because it was right above the boiler room, all my friends joked about the opportunity I was missing by not holding hot yoga classes on the living room's unforgiving Berber carpet. I borrowed an industrial fan and took to only wearing bikinis. Unlike the basement suite, this place had large alley-facing windows that framed a colony of fighting jackrabbits. I watched them and knew that the people walking by outside could see my half-naked self. I waved to them from the linoleum of my own private beach and, sometimes, they waved back.

One afternoon, while helping my only nearby neighbour with her groceries, I learned she was deaf. I could play my music as loud as I liked, and nobody would say a thing. I spent my nights cooking noxious vegan stews, full of bright green cruciferous vegetables that stank up the apartment. I kept all the windows open, despite the snow falling outside. There was no one to tell me to close them. I let the music blare, and danced around the apartment, my bikini bottoms riding up my hips. Alone at last, and glad to be that way.

"If you won't sleep with me,
why do I even have a bed?"

In the Land of the Strangler Fig

I HAD BEEN LOSING my faith for some time, the way you misplace items you'd once thought crucial but realize you can get along without. The final straw broke the night my church mentor and her husband had sex on the bed next to me. As she gripped my arm, pinning me to the mattress, she had dispersed those last ghosts of belief in an interventionist god.

Afterwards, I tried to blend into the city I'd just moved to, hoping to make my past seem less obvious. I tittered with new girlfriends about a musician we all liked who supposedly slept with a friend of a friend whenever he came through for a gig.

"I'd love to kiss him," I gushed.

There was a beat of silence before one of the girls said, "You know he's not the kind of guy that you just 'kiss,' right?"

I said I did, but this was a lie. All the sex I'd experienced had been in that darkened bedroom with my eyes shut tight.

I believed, if I could just get out ahead of the things that might happen to me, if I could do them to myself first, they wouldn't hurt me because I would see them coming the next time around. So, weeks after the assault with my church mentor, I followed a girlfriend and the boss she was sleeping with to a swinger's club.

Upon our arrival, my friend tied me to a St. Andrew's Cross—an x-shaped apparatus that allowed the person attached to it to be secured in a spread-eagle position—and left me there like an offering in a low-lit room filled with strangers. Supposedly, when St. Andrew was crucified, he thought himself unworthy of being martyred on the same equipment as Jesus, hence the titling of his cross.

Standing in the darkness, I noticed the eyeshine of strangers as their gazes flitted to me. I could hear my friend and her paramour somewhere behind me: slack skin slapping against slack skin. Soon, a woman came up and kissed me on the lips. "You're beautiful," she said, "both my husband and I think so." Then, she seemed to notice my duress. "Do you want me to let you down from there?" she asked.

"Please."

I fell against her. My hands and feet bloodless from being tied too tight. The couple invited me home with them, but I declined, content to stay and feel the pins-and-needles burn in the tips of my appendages.

The club had lost its liquor licence some months prior, and the wine I'd drunk beforehand was wearing off. One of the bouncers lounged on a chaise made of black leather with me, his thick fingers playing across the steel bones of the corset I wore. I ignored him until he produced a silver flask from beneath his leather jacket. I sipped from it, and the whiskey inside had just the right amount of burn. I turned onto my belly and watched as the deflated cherry tattoo on a woman's backside dipped and surfaced again, beneath a slick pile of naked bodies. My brain tried and failed to name the things in front of me: that's a dick, that's a shoe, that's a hand grenade.

Men darted around me, monstrous in their nudity. They required a female escort to remain on this level of the club, and I was alone. But already I was tired of their advances. I had envisioned a headache-inducing sort of desire, drug-like in its potency. Yet I felt nothing. I was already learning: sex that you didn't want was the same everywhere.

I left those smashing bodies behind and stepped out the back door into the cooling winter night. Beneath a dark and silent sky, the woman with the cherry tattoo sidled up to me. Her hand went to my hair, sweeping it back from my face. I expected her fingers to trail down to the tops of my breasts. There had been a sort of permission inside the club, as if, with the waivers that we had signed at the door, we had already consented to everything that might happen. Instead, she stopped at my chin and pulled her hand away.

"You remind me so much of my daughter," the woman said. "She's sixteen and I just don't have control of her at all."

To my surprise, tears beaded up in the corners of her eyes. When the girl who'd brought me to the club came looking, she found me still out back, puffing menthol cigarettes from a pack the cherry-woman shared, my arm around her, her anguish knitting us together.

I did find desire after that night, but in someone who did not share the feeling. Then, there was a man who felt it while I did not. He showed me that to some men, this was of little consequence. I told his sister, a close friend, what had happened, and she and I went out to drink the memory away. At the end of the evening, she drove me back to him, and this time I acquiesced, because what did it matter now?

Just as it had been in the church, I found myself trampled. I thought perhaps the problem was me, that I could never become someone else if I didn't write myself into a new character, a new story, a new setting. So, I boarded a series of flights that took me all the way to Bangkok.

When I stepped out of the airport, the sudden blast of humidity soaked into me. I piled into a van with several other people, and from the back window, I watched the shimmering lights of a thousand homes rush by. It looked like the sky was inverted, because the pollution above us had blacked out the stars.

While I walked on Khao San Road, I pondered my own anonymity. I didn't have to tell anyone here that I'd once been so devout that I had been baptized twice. I didn't even have to use my real name. That night, I sat in an open-air bar drinking until morning. I watched as the other patrons milled about getting to know each other, seeming sure of themselves and their own skins. I hardly spoke, too afraid that if I did, I'd give myself away.

The teeming, bloated city was just as I'd hoped it would be. At night, you could get lost in a crush of people and liquor. The markets were a blur of lighted signs and fried food, the flames of the sizzling woks signaling to the drunks like beacons. Fake driver's licences were sold beside the stalls of men giving real tattoos. Marilyn Monroe's almost recognizable face rendered permanent on the fleshy meat of someone's thigh.

I heard tell of Ping Pong shows, exhibitions where women fired the little white balls out of their vaginas, and sometimes, razor blades that cut cleanly through hanging sheets of paper. There were even women who smoked out of that most intimate of orifices. Men in tuk-tuks (those little golf-cart-like-vehicles that sped along the roadways) approached me. They made popping noises with their mouths, the universal advertisement for a Ping Pong show. And I, embarrassed, flushed and ducked into yet another bar.

During the daylight hours, the city became something else. On the hottest afternoons, I'd often go to the air-conditioned theatres, where the national anthem was played before each film. We stood in front of our seats, one hand on our popcorn and the other over our hearts in a show of reverence to the king. For the more devout, there were the temples. Their spires were scattered throughout the city: golden points of brilliance alongside the bland concrete boxes of malls and office buildings.

"You know," a man I met later in my trip told me, "many of the temples are built on the backs of prostitutes, especially those in the villages. The girls come home and buy absolution in the shape of swan-dragons. All these beautiful sacred things, funded from the spoils of sex."

When Bangkok's endless, brightly lighted nights became too much, I followed a tour group to the southern islands of the country. The towers and overpasses dropped away, revealing bamboo bridges and rickety bungalows, structures that looked like the bones of the places we had just been.

On a beach in Ko Pha Ngan, I met an American man. He'd developed some part of the oil refining process that afforded him the ability to leave the United States behind for good. He'd been on this same island for eight years now, dropping acid, his visa so long expired that he could no longer calculate the fines he was sure to receive if he tried to go home again.

"But," he assured me, "I can pay them, whatever they are."

The American and I drank together on St. Patrick's Day, in the company of two Irishmen celebrating their recent release from prison following a dropped drug charge. I remember little about that night, only that the two Irishmen had the same first name. In the morning, I woke to find the dress I'd left my bungalow in the night before gone. Instead, I wore only bathing suit bottoms and a Thai police officer's vest. I wish I could tell you how this happened, but I simply don't remember.

The tour group left for another beach, and I opted to stay behind. In the company of a Norwegian DJ, I visited a bar on the island where you could order numbered items off a plastic menu—like a late-night Chinese-food place—except the numbers corresponded to different drugs. The DJ bought hash with what I think was opium mixed in, and we headed into the jungle. We passed a stairway crafted from bottles pushed into the dirt. To me, it seemed as if their green and brown glass was lit-up from within. At the top of the stairway, we stumbled on a Muay Thai ring shaded by a dense canopy of banyan trees—those strangler figs. I gawked and daydreamed of men circling each other, the fabric of their silvery shorts jiggling as they bounced from foot-to-foot.

I heard voices, and the DJ and I burst through the trees into a space filled with people. He ate a bowl of soup while I picked at my fingernails. It was too bright in that place. I was too high to withstand the buzzing din. At last, he took my hand and we left, disappearing again into the welcome quiet of the trees.

We ended up sitting on the beach until first light. I watched the waves as they churned in on themselves and then unfurled onto the sand in what looked like writhing masses of snakes. I peered at them from between the gaps in my fingers. Still, they were snakes.

The following day, the DJ and I went into that water. We were already up to our waists when he admitted, "I'm not the best swimmer."

"Well, I am," I reassured him.

We let the waves take us out. When the bottom dropped away, he panicked. It turned out he couldn't swim at all. "Put your hands on my shoulders," I coaxed, as I focused on propelling us towards shore. It felt like we'd only spent moments in the water, but the current had already pulled us a great distance out, the sunbathers in the sand were specks on the horizon. I kept the Norwegian's back to the beach.

"We're going to be okay," I told him, the fear bright as a lightning strike in his eyes.

But I could feel myself dipping below the water, my legs cramping with exhaustion. A clarity came over me, and I understood we were not going to make it back. There was no fear with this realization, only resignation. I started to go under, and my kicking foot touched down on the grit of sand.

As we scuttled up onto the beach, I admonished him, "There's a big difference between being a bad swimmer and being unable to do it at all."

He seemed not to hear me and said, "I knew a guy that drowned in that same spot a few years ago. It's deeper on this side of the beach, and harder to get back in again."

"You knew," I sputtered. It occurred to me only then I could still get hurt here, that I could still die. I'd been thinking of this place as a reprieve from reality, a sort of simulation. As if nothing I did here mattered.

When I woke again, disorientated and a little sick, I was snuggled into the Norwegian's bed. He'd been watching me sleep for a long while, the pulled slivers of sunburnt skin around me evidence of the time that had passed.

A few days later, he left without saying goodbye. I set up a hammock outside my bungalow and watched the man in the neighbouring bungalow light a crack pipe every hour or so, the flare of the lighter like a pendulum strike on the strangest of clocks. My neighbour was friendly and offered me a hit several times. I considered it but had a feeling it was something I might not come back from.

Soon, I peeled myself from the hammock, the latticework of its ropes having cut deep grooves into my legs, and caught up with the tour group and took a boat to the full moon party in Hat Rin. At the party, I flitted about the edges, mostly sober, watching as couples had sex in the water and drunks pissed in the same ocean a few feet away. Everything was on fire. Girls jumped over flaming skipping ropes and men paused to light their cigarettes as they limboed under burning poles. The air was thick with the smell of diesel fuel. Strangers staggered past, their skin illuminated with glowing paint, cheekbones and cleavage outlined in neon. They looked like patients undergoing medical tests, radio active dye shot beneath their skin to show rapidly multiplying clusters of cells.

Most of the people on the tour had taken MDMA, but I opted out. A girl I'd become friends with stumbled about, her pupils poured over the blue of her irises, staining them like ink. I watched her climb the ladder of a slide with its sides on fire. At the top, she caught her foot between a gap in two concrete blocks. She was too high to feel the pain when she pulled it free, too high to notice she had snapped her own shin.

In the morning, the equatorial sun bolted into the sky. It burned our exposed skins and illuminated a beach awash in garbage. Under its light, the girl with the broken shinbone began to sober up, to feel the wrongness of the bone in her leg. She and I made our way to the first long-tail boat we saw. The helmsman took pity on us and helped me haul her quaking body aboard. The doctor she would see later that day misdiagnosed the seriousness of her injury. It had to be broken again when she arrived home in Canada.

The tour group left Ko Pha Ngan for another island. Not long after our departure, a major earthquake and tsunami hit Japan, sending shockwaves all through the Pacific Ocean. Most of the bungalows we'd stayed in had fallen away into the sea. It felt as if everything I'd done was washing away behind me, my sins blotted out by acts of God.

Now we were stranded. Nothing could move through the rough water, the storms and heavy rains grounding all boats. I partied in the rain, thinking of Noah, of animals traveling two-by-two. Beneath a sky burst open, a young man's hands encircled the thinnest part of my waist, that place where I fold like a letter. The young man and I ducked into a covered long-tail boat to kiss. Beneath us, the craft rocked with the crashing waves, knocking our teeth together and making us laugh. Suddenly, there was a man squatting on the boat's prow. His stance was gargoyle-like, and the dim moonlight cast monstrous shadows across the planes of his tired face.

"No boom-boom in my boat," he said.

From his tone, I could tell we were not the first to be caught doing such a thing. I scuttled out, the young man trailing me, the colour-bloom of shame on my cheeks obscured by the deluge of falling water.

The young man walked me back to my hotel, our clothes slick against our wet skins. I kept my body away from his now, all desire leached from me. At the door of my room, he asked to come in and use the bathroom. I let him, and he emerged naked a moment later. He was much drunker than I was, so it was easy to shove him out into the hall, tossing his clothes out after him.

In the morning, I had breakfast with some of the girls who'd been at the bar with me the night before. They'd seen me leave with the young man and laughed at how my night had turned out.

"That guy tried his hand with all of us," the most sunburned girl said, between sips of her breakfast beer. "We couldn't believe it when you went off with him. You should have checked in with us before you left, we would have told you he was a scumbag."

In my head, there were women holding me down in their beds, and women giving me to their brothers, and women tying me to crosses and leaving me vulnerable. I could no longer be sure of which of them to trust. In front of me, the sunburned girl said something.

"Sorry, what was that?"

"I asked if you were okay."

"I'm fine," I replied, "just fine."

But I was not fine. It took me stumbling across a journal entry from that night, years later, to remember what had really happened. As I pushed the young man towards the door, he had managed to fish a hand up my dress, his fingers catching painfully on the inside of me like a hook.

When the storms calmed, the tour group moved on to the island of Ko Lanta. On that beach at night, wiry men twirled lengths of heavy chain lit on fire, plumes of light blooming in the black sky above them. Nearby, a woman swallowed swords beneath the glow. The metal flashed as it caught the reflection of the firelight and then disappeared into the opened maw of her throat.

In front of the bungalow where I was staying, a hibiscus bush grew in a fuchsia riot. I hung my hammock high above its foliage. The gardener came each day to trim the plant until it was nothing but spikey nubs in the dirt beneath me. A few nights into my time in that place, I padded out the door of my bungalow into the total darkness of the late evening. Just as the motion-light switched off above me, the gardener stepped out of the shadows. His hands closed tight around the flesh of my upper arms. I didn't even think. I shoved him backwards with the heels of my hands, into the sharp fronds of the very bush he'd cut down to nothing.

Then I ran.

In the lighted place of the resort restaurant, I found the girl with the broken shin, now hobbled by crutches.

"Are you alright?" she asked me, seeing the panic on my face.

I shook my head and told her what had happened beneath the buzzing hum of the dozen fans that whirred above us.

"Come on," she coaxed gently.

I followed her with my arms crossed protectively over my chest, my hands resting just below the spots where the bruises of fingertips would bloom the next day.

"You shouldn't have been so friendly," the tour coordinator scolded me when we found him.

"I said hello to him every day, and that was all," I defended myself.

"We'll sort it out in the morning," he said, "in the meantime, I'm going out."

That night, I stayed with the girl with the broken shin, huddled beside her in a room full of the sounds of other women breathing. By morning, the tour coordinator had taken care of things, in a way. The gardener was a relative of the hotel owner. He would be talked to, and that would be all. After that, I split from the group.

I took a bus north, and that was where I first met Noel, the man who told me about temples built on the backs of prostitutes. It was an image that made me think of women weighted down with gilded shells: human-turtle hybrids. For the next three years, Noel would pop in and out of my life, the two of us flying across continents to see each other. Over those years, I would view him as my guide and guru, though I didn't know then that's what I was doing. That I still believed I needed to worship at the feet of someone.

Noel was interested in desolation, and he wanted to show it to me: the dusty red canyons of Thailand, scattered with tiny villages where the locals steamed in the heat that came off the mountains. We took a motor bike to the northern tip of that country, into the middle of nowhere. His search of the vast countryside was an ever-widening one. Under a crisp, blue sky, we made our way to lonelier places, to older ruins and to where there were fewer people who looked like us.

I remember those dirt roads so well, seated on the back of his bike as a hill tribe woman tried to wave us down to sell us opium, a baby strapped to her chest and the bells on her clothes jangling. It seemed absurd for her to be out in the heat in traditional dress. Her heavy clothes—with their stripes of pinks and greens and blues stitched onto a black background, vibrant pom poms dangling from every hem—were a pop of colour against the otherwise barren-looking landscape.

When Noel had to return to Australia, I followed another group of backpackers onto a slow boat. For two days, we drifted across the Mekong River and into Laos. There, the word for water was the same as it had been in Thailand. But everything else had shifted just enough to be confusing, as I reached for the word I'd known and caught myself just in time. I could see that the two languages had the same root, like a plant whose seeds had carried on the wind to somewhere new and adapted to the conditions of that place's soil.

The most glaring difference was that Laos was communist while Thailand was not. News and social media sites had to be rerouted through proxy servers, the site names passed through backpackers like a game of telephone. There were many fuzzy mornings spent sitting over a keyboard and trying to remember what I'd been told last night after several beers, the innocent act of talking to my mother via social media made to seem odd and clandestine.

I moved on from the tiny port town of Chiang Khong to the French architecture of Luang Prabang, where breakfast came served on a baguette. After that, it was on to Vang Vieng, a tiny town in a pocket of the country left alone by the government. You could drink in the streets at any hour of the day. And late at night, you'd see clusters of local men tailing the drunkest girls, their moon-faces unaware of the leering conga-line behind them. Every one of the open-air restaurants on the main strip played re-runs of *Friends.* In my memories of that place, Rachel's tousled shag is forever in the background.

One morning while I was there, three English girls made the paper for showing up in their swimwear to Rong Khun Temple in Chiang Rai, Thailand. When I had stopped in at that sacred place on my way to Laos, I had stepped gingerly over the walkway into the temple, where a sea of white plaster hands reached up from below, as if to grab you and pull you down with them. I'd laughed about the English girls' lack of reverence along with everybody else, though I knew I wasn't much better.

When I had visited, I'd forgotten that it was only polite to cover one's knees while in a sacred space. I'd worn shorts and, my head downcast in shame, had to sling a borrowed sarong around my hips before I headed inside. I too was a foreigner or, a Farang, as a little girl had yelled at me once in the street while the men on either side of her laughed. The locals used the same word for guava, that green, pocked immigrant fruit that didn't quite belong.

The division between locals and tourists was made starker because about half of us had bandages snaking up our limbs, as if it were a fashion statement. It was surreal to sit on the bus next to Chinese tourists who travelled in wedding dresses and ball gowns. These gilded women slept open-mouthed, the gemstones on their collars sticking out like broken bones. In the streets, the long fabric of their skirts spooled out behind scooters, their jewel-toned gowns looking like tropical birds in flight. But by nightfall, there was always talk of another accident, of fabric caught in bike wheels. I'd see the same girls the next day, now in jeans, thick white bandages covering their arms.

We were all moving so fast. Each night was like a possibility of a death, someone exiting from your life by morning. And maybe that person had been as close to your soulmate as you were ever going to get. I was wild as anything, high, and stupid, and probably wanting to die more than a little bit.

One night, I'd gone out to the local bars with a Welshman I'd met on the slow boat from Thailand to Laos. We drank from liquor bottles in the street, some bartender pouring it straight down our throats. We kissed, passing melting ice cubes back and forth between our mouths.

Afterwards, we'd made our way across the bridge over the Nam Song River, to where a red-headed Englishman served us plastic sand pails filled to the brim with magic mushrooms. I ate them until the faces of the people around me started to shift into cartoon mice and rats from the graphic novel I'd been reading. The Welshman and I stood on top of a picnic table letting the drugs take hold of us, as a sea of other backpackers flowed past our feet. A young woman stopped to say that we looked like gods to her and in that moment, I felt convinced of my own immortality.

We made our way back over the bridge towards the main strip, pausing with another couple to see a bright, glowing caterpillar that shambled across the ground. One of the temples was still open, and I sat outside while the Welshman went in to pray, his beer left behind on the front step. In the garden, I watched the statues of Buddha shift into Power Rangers. I lifted my eyes to the sky, which still looked blue to me despite the lateness of the hour. The lights from the nearby homes and hotels glittered in that blueness, like boats on a sea. When I looked in on the Welshman a few minutes later, his beautiful face was almost kissing the temple floor.

We'd gone searching for my hotel after that, a monu mental task under the weight of the drugs, though the town had only two main streets. When we finally found the building, it took us hours to get up to my room because we stopped to dance on each floor, both of us fighting to lead as he sang what he said was an old Welsh song. The designs of the tiles swirled beneath our bare feet. I remember how ugly I thought his feet were, and that they seemed incongruent on such a beautiful man. At the door of my room, I kissed the Welshman goodnight and then I went to bed alone. I never saw him again.

When I ran across the friend who'd been traveling with the Welshman a while later, I found out the friend hadn't seen him either. A faint sort of concern showed on his face. Someone else told me the missing man had been an opium addict. Maybe he was in a den somewhere and had lost track of time like the soldiers we'd heard about from a nearby war who'd never gone home. If you know a Welshman with his nickname tattooed along the instep of his foot in Thai, please let him know I still worry about him.

The day after my mushroom adventure, I linked up with some girls I'd met along the way and went tubing down the river. Rickety bamboo bars stippled the banks. Locals and tourists alike would pull your tube to the side of the waterway and serve you beers and tequila shots. The liquor built up your courage for the steepness of the slides that fed straight down into the water and the clusters of rocks hidden beneath its surface. That year, twenty-seven people would die in Vang Vieng in tubing-related deaths.

At first, the river was jammed up with people. Screaming backpackers kicked dirty water at each other. The little covered bars were tightly crammed together and seemed to go on forever. Then, they thinned out and finally disappeared, leaving us to float alone until we came upon a group of cows cooling themselves in the water. They looked at us lazily and we decided to pull out and walk back to the main road.

I left Southeast Asia not long after. I had kept in touch with Noel because I had liked the way he'd showed me things. I visited him in Australia for a short time, after which I went home.

This time in my life is a geographic blur. I was without a fixed address, the mail and fines I was accruing returned to sender. When I look over my journals from this time, it seems as if I'm writing while on a flight every third page or so, my life and words constantly in motion. It felt right at the time, but perhaps it was just distraction that I craved.

Back in Canada, I still had too many things I was seeking to settle back into my life as it had been. I was looking for someone to stumble through with me, to experiment with and to trust.

Noel and I met up a second time a few months later in Northern Thailand, where we threaded up and into the mountains once more. We sped about on roads so steeply curving that we often saw buses flung to the sides of them: overturned and with the detritus of those who'd once been inside now scattered through the nearby forest. North and north and north we went to the very tip of that place. It was as if we were trying to launch ourselves into the sky, to hook the moon with the tires of our bike.

Tiring of the journey, we began to work our way back to Vang Vieng. The town was beautiful, Noel explained, not for its sullied river, but for its waterfalls. We would return, but this time we would do it right. When we arrived, tubing was still going on and parties filled the streets, but there were fewer people now. Bars along the river were getting shut down and the government had gotten involved. No one wanted to be from the place tourists went to die. The locals had begun avoiding the river too, that once life-giving place. Now it was seen only as a source of bad luck.

Noel and I stayed outside of town and rented a scooter that we took to the nearby waterfalls. As we climbed on the rocks and watched the water cascade down into perfectly clear pools, I thought of how different it was out here, how quiet. In the sweeping coolness that came with dusk, I ran along the blacktop of an abandoned airstrip outside the town, a decommissioned holdover from the Vietnam War. It was only me and another girl circling that strip of pavement. We sprinted in opposite directions, nodding to each other each time we crossed paths. As my feet slapped the surface of the earth, I thought about all the things I didn't know.

I didn't know how to be better to myself, or to ask that others be better to me. I was too busy looking for stories of my own to tell, rather than how to get home without getting hurt. I felt this lapse every time I chewed, the grinding of my jaw sounding a warning. It was the place where Noel had punched me while we were in bed together. I'd told him to hit me, but I'd expected an open hand. A bit of play. Not a closed fist and the stars that exploded across my vision when it hit.

On one of our last nights there, Noel and I entered an Indian restaurant and settled into the pile of embroidered pillows on the floor. Across the room, we saw a young man with long red hair who was resting on his elbows next to a pretty girl. On his leg there was a long, uncovered gash. The wound was green in the restaurant light. I looked over at Noel, and though we were usually the type to keep to ourselves, he walked over to the young man and asked if he'd been to a doctor about the gangrenous gash. The young man had smiled, not bothered by our interruption to his meal.

"Yes," he replied, "I've been to a doctor. He prescribed me antibiotics, but I just can't stop drinking long enough to take them. And every day I go back to swim in the river, even though I know I shouldn't. I'm flying home to Australia at the end of the week. I'll have it seen to when I'm back."

We wished him good luck, but I remember being afraid for him. The cut had looked much worse than others I'd seen, some of which had to be scraped out to leave a deep hollow in the flesh.

When I went to Australia about a year afterwards, I looked for the man with the cut on his leg. In Flinders Street Station, I thought I saw him once. But it was someone else, this man's long hair rust-brown instead of red, the metal of the prosthetic leg showing beneath the hem of his shorts, glinting and bright in the Melbourne sun.

Ghost Shirt

In Bangkok, everything stayed open late. While still hazy with jetlag, I had to squint in the too-bright fluorescent lights of the shops. I circled around huge aquariums, my mouth agape at the sight of whiskery fish and crustaceans that seemed as if they had too many claws. I felt like a sleepwalker who'd just been woken by the stinking pile of durians at my left. Signs in front of certain hotels declared the spikey, too-pungent fruit banned inside. In Thailand, I was often called beautiful, but I suspected it was only the colour of my skin that made the women say so. I sometimes stood beneath a shop awning, trying to hide from the sun, as the bolder among them flocked to me, asking if they could touch me, stroking my arms and saying "khao" over and over. Literally, "white."

In the boxes of truck taxis, I watched women hold their pocketbooks over the backs of their exposed necks, worried the rays from the windows would brown the small patch of skin that showed. In the malls, young girls covered their faces so thickly with white powder that when they smiled, they looked like porcelain dolls cracking. In the drugstores, I hunted for lotion and deodorant that did not contain bleaching agents. I had bought the latter by mistake once, and only noticed after the flaking skin under my armpits turned the colour of powdered sugar.

Outwardly, I called this obsession with whiteness foolish, but anyone could see I too had bought in. It showed in the long-sleeved shirts I now wore despite the heat, in the climbing digits of my SPF, and in the ever-widening brims of my hats and umbrellas. I felt regal and witchy beneath the shade, strolling along in a circle of shadow, like a tiny disc of night beneath the unrelenting sun.

Under the colourful awnings of Chatuchak's weekend market, on the edges of the city, the stalls stretched on for miles. If I saw something I liked, I'd been advised by fellow travellers to buy it, because I'd never find it again. In front of me, towers of textiles loomed in a technicolour maze. I can still remember how tightly I kept my Australian boyfriend Noel's hand crushed inside of mine. Like all those other things I admired, I worried, if we lost sight of each other, that I would never find him again.

Worldliness was what I was hoping to learn from Noel. He'd been coming to Thailand for years by the time we met, staying so long that most of his accent was gone, leaving behind only a slight elongation on some vowels—not enough even for a clue towards his country of origin. Meanwhile, I understood that it was my youth he coveted. I was twenty-two and he was thirty. We joked about when he would leave me for a younger model. My pet name for him came from a Japanese cartoon of a pedophiliac bear, while his for me was from Nabokov.

Inside Chatuchak, the fabrics gave way to hanging lights, a million paper globes dotting the temporary ceiling like dwarf planets; then tarps where the rows of animals began. Tiny windows of glass showed fish, their ruffled fins lit-up in a fireworks display of injected neon dye. Hands that looked like my own gripped bars, the slats between them revealing the flat faces of monkeys. Other cages held creatures I couldn't even attempt to name. Some had billowing parachutes of skin under their arms, and others huge swivelling eyes that dominated their trapped faces. They all seemed impossibly wild, as if they'd just been snatched from the jungle moments ago, as foreign to the city's paved streets as I was to this place.

At home, I might forget a thing or two when I went to run errands, but in the markets of Bangkok, I often forgot why I had come at all. As the day bled into night, a tattoo shop rolled out its awning, the photos under its cover showing the Sak Yant tattoos belonging to Angelina Jolie: the tiger and the five lines. The five lines tattoo (also known as the five Yants) was everywhere. Locals and travellers wanted the blessings that came with it—among them, were success and attraction of the opposite sex. And perhaps it worked, for a time. Back then, I fell asleep at night looking at it on Noel's shoulder.

I preferred the smaller places, they were less overwhelming, less a bombardment of all the things I hadn't seen and didn't know and possibly never would. Being from a small town, with an education that bore the gaps religion dictated, I was aware I might never convincingly pretend I fit somewhere bigger. And I did need to pretend. I'd begun to understand that most people wouldn't allow you to catch up. They'd just take advantage of your greenness.

So it was a relief when Noel and I stepped away from the city, winding our way up into the mountains of the province of Mae Hong Son, and back to the town of Pai where we'd first met the year before. Once settled in that sparsely populated region, I found it easier to breathe, even with the garlic burning in the nearby hills, the blackened sky turning the sun an apocalyptic red.

In Pai, the markets were more compact, not so easy to get lost in. Though the stalls were crammed with curious combinations of things: little one-stop-shops with displays of kitchen knives and wireless speakers propped on cages of live chickens. The women who ran the stalls seemed supernatural in their wide-brimmed hats, their gloved hands pressed together as if in prayer, clasping the money they'd just received from the day's first sale, swatting it gently against the wares on their tables in a methodical good-luck ritual that resembled some spell only they knew the steps to.

Though smaller, these markets were still an apex of local nightlife. Out behind the stalls, there were cockfights and boxing rings. The kids who practiced Muay Thai inside the rings were sometimes as young as eight. Watching them, I squirmed. Legs connecting hard against flesh, a kicked-out-shin striking a jaw full of baby teeth.

"It's what they do," Noel assured me. "It's what they've always done."

In another ring, I watched fierce boys of no more than sixteen circle each other. Identical Hanuman tattoos peeked out from the bottoms of their shorts, as if the venerable monkey warrior had come along to weigh in on the outcome of their fights.

After the matches ended, we'd always head to a bar. I flash back sometimes to one night in particular at a place outside of town. While we were there, Noel got so drunk I couldn't even look at him. I wanted to leave but he kept insisting on one last beer. Finally, I took off alone. It was the middle of the night by then, the sky a moonless black. The walk back to our guesthouse was a long one, but I knew the way.

A dog began to follow me, matching the speed of his steps to mine. At first, he was welcome company, but then another joined us, and another. I realized the animals were strays and they were hungry. They howled for their brethren until half-a-dozen or so trailed behind me. I didn't turn around to count them, only waited to feel teeth on the back of my neck.

And then I heard the bikes. The dogs scattered like a wave breaking apart. Suddenly in my right periphery, there were two men astride one bike, and a third riding alone on his own machine. As if mirroring the dogs' behaviour, they slowed when I slowed, ditto when I picked up the pace. I still remember wondering which would be worse: to be torn apart by wild dogs or whatever these men intended to do to me.

Another bike peeled up on my left side, surrounding me. I turned my head to see how many men it was carrying, but it was only Turtle, an acquaintance of Noel's I'd met a few days before.

"Do you need a ride?" he asked, as if there was nothing strange at all about the situation he'd found me in, though his eyes were wild behind his glasses.

"Please," I said into the back of his shirt, for I'd already climbed onto his bike and we were speeding away, the wind peeling my hair free of the fear sweat that had licked it to my scalp.

The next morning, I found Noel asleep on a chair on the veranda of our guesthouse, having forgotten his keys.

"You could have knocked," I said.

"I didn't want to wake you. I knew you were already furious with me last night."

"I was," I admitted, leaving the door to our bungalow open behind me as I took off in search of breakfast without him. I didn't bother to tell him about the men or the dogs. He was my guide, but never my protector.

Some nights, Noel and I played pool with sex workers in dimly lit bars while they waited for customers. Meanwhile others in the same trade stood in front of massage parlors, calling out "you want happy ending?" or the less titillating but just as breathily spoken "massage?" The bodies of the bolder of them folding at the waist into Noel, stopping him in his tracks. All of it seemed obscene to me until I began to understand the many reasons for it.

I learned that some of those around me were mid-transition, while others had finished with it, the change so seamless in a sequinned gown that I wouldn't have known of it had they not told me. Though it did not come without difficulty. Trans persons could not change their genders on their ID cards, leading to discrimination in the job market. Our friend Amanda, who self-identified as a ladyboy, was blunt about the situation.

"We are either forced to become prostitutes or thieves," she declared. "I'm proud to consider myself part of the second group."

I couldn't fathom the danger in this occupation. In Thailand, if born male, even if fully transitioned, you still went to men's prison.

I was from the sort of place where, a few years after I took this trip, a local gay man would be beaten to death in front of a crowd of onlookers. The man's assailant would blame the murder on the unwanted attention his victim had shown him. There was no allowing for any sort of deviation from the expected genders or the trajectories of their desires, never mind the eighteen combinations Thailand recognized. It would be a long time before I could admit what I wanted—that just because I was drunk didn't mean the things I sometimes did with women in the back seats of cars didn't count. It was a small thing, compared to our

Thai friends' struggle, though it seemed colossal to me in that moment of my life.

I grew grateful that there were indications of identity right in the Thai language. If you chose to present yourself as female, a polite "ka" was added at the end of every sentence, if male, you inserted a "krap," though no gender-neutral option existed. I didn't understand how you could be sure enough of who you were that you could announce it even in your speech patterns.

In Pai, Noel introduced me to an Israeli trans woman. Some years before, while doing her mandatory military service in her home country, she'd stolen the hormones she needed and dosed herself, guessing. She had been employed as a sex worker afterwards. It was common knowledge around the little mountain town that she had beaten a violent client within an inch of his life. She could no longer go home; criminal charges awaited her there. Now, she lived in a sort of stateless limbo with a woman from one of the local hill tribes that she'd physically removed from a relationship with an abusive husband. When I met the Israeli woman, I'd hardly said a word. I was too in awe of her own self-possession to speak.

I saw the two of them around town afterwards, the hill tribe woman perched on the back of the other woman's bike, their hair flung out behind them in the wind: one's inky black and the other a frizzing corona of blonde curl beneath a tied kerchief.

Noel had known the Israeli woman for years, having stayed long enough to cement himself with the locals.

He'd even built a bar in a nearby community even more rural than Pai, and become friendly with his landlord. Later, Noel introduced me to that man and his friends, all of whom were farmers. Following their lead, we walked through jungles, balancing on steep edges carved into the hillsides over dams, trying not to look down into the gullies below. We strode through rivers where the farmers showed us how to stun fish using a car battery. Some of the silvery, shocked bodies of their catch still thrashed as they rose to the surface, the scaled bellies of those that were already dead glinting like coins in the sunlight.

Hours into the trek, I would notice the bumps that ran up and down my legs and itched terribly. Jungle bites, the farmers called them. No one else had even one. The farmers said it was the colour of my flesh that had called to the bugs like a beacon as we stepped through the murk of the waist-deep river.

On these hikes, the farmers paused to carve full sets of dishes out of bamboo and shared their meals. I was a vegetarian, and they were kind about this, seeing it as some sort of Buddhist devotion. Meanwhile, Noel noshed iguana liver, a pinky-grey meat that made his kisses taste of metal for days afterward. There were also bowls of snake soup that I was happy to sit out, the animal coiled in the pot the same one we'd seen felled an hour before with a slingshot. The farmers shared fruit with me, and the thimble-sized eggs of some unknown animal, the yolks impossibly yellow. Between bites, we sipped Lao Khao, the local rice whiskey. The whiskey came in reused plastic pop bottles or tiny clear bags—the sort of thing you'd take a pet goldfish home in. And sure enough, after the bag was empty your eyes swam.

We'd think of all these things we'd consumed a month or so later, while visiting the Siriraj Medical Museum in Bangkok. Down a twisting corridor, Noel and I had been alone in rooms of preserved conjoined twins and swollen-headed babies that had died of hydrocephalus. The percolating scent of formaldehyde was overwhelming in the Thai heat. Tattooed, unattached limbs and lone organs bobbed in the liquid.

In the main area, the mummified body of alleged serial killer Si Quey stood in a glass case, the bullet holes in him still visible despite the five decades since his death. It was years after our visit before activists successfully lobbied to have his remains cremated, his guilt of murdering and cannibalizing several children largely disputed. For so long, he'd been the country's boogeyman. "Be good, or Si Quey will come eat you," was the common warning from Thai parents. And when I saw him behind the glass, I'd stared as if these were only the remains of some animal, unaware that it was likely anti-Chinese, anti-Communist sentiment that caused his death by firing squad at the age of thirty-two.

Near Si Quey's body, there was a replica of a testicle grown huge from elephantiasis. Though usually spread by mosquitos, the explanation below the hulking sex organ claimed the parasite could be picked up from eating certain uncooked foods. Many of those listed were the same things the farmers had been sharing with Noel. After the museum, we sat at a restaurant on the shores of the Chao

Phraya River. We toasted each other with bottles of Tiger beer, intertwining our arms as we fed each other identical de-worming pills, the huge white tablets sticking in our throats.

My Thai was bad, my pronunciations so confusing that Noel asked me to stop trying on our outings with the farmers. After he did so, I became purely decorative: the young white thing in the corner who didn't talk. Still, I couldn't help but cling to the few things I did know. Above all, I loved that the direct translation of the Thai word for "butterfly" was "ghost shirt."

Noel was proficient enough to translate the farmers' jokes. In them, I soon noticed a pattern. The farmers always begged off before it got too late, saying they had to get home before their wives had something to feed to the ducks. This would draw a raucous fit of laughter from the other men. When I asked Noel why this was so funny later, he explained that it was relatively common for Thai women to sever their partners' penises. They would then throw the offending organ out the window to the milling livestock outside. I didn't believe him until I went online and found dozens of articles about this practice, with one particularly memorable woman who'd attached her cheating husband's penis to a helium balloon and sent it up, up and away.

Eventually, we left Pai behind and boarded a bus headed for Cambodia. The road between the two countries was under construction, the crossing a serpentine horror of potholed switchbacks. Only an hour in, we had to pull over. I stood huddled in a circle of women with whom I shared not a scrap of language. We didn't need it though. Instead, we held hands or pulled back the tails of each others' hair as we took turns vomiting into a nearby ditch.

Not long after our arrival in Siem Reap, Noel and I ventured out to see the temples of Angkor Wat. We left our hotel before sunrise, hoping to catch the first rays of day-light as it spread out over the temple spires. But the sky was overcast, the cloying pollution of the nearby city blotting out the cresting sunlight.

Together, Noel and I puzzled over the temple ground signs: we were to wear shirts and not talk loudly. Pregnant women were not allowed. This was odd to us, given the number of statues of the Yoni and Linga, those fertility symbols of Shiva and Shakti. We averted our eyes from the women bowing low to them, giving them their privacy as they prayed for the standing water to become a wellspring of fecundity.

There were signs of decay everywhere. Much of the Ta Prohm temple had been worn away by the jutting trunks of trees. The Tetrameles, sometimes called chicken-foot trees, used their clawed-feet to grip the ancient structure in a slow-climb. On the face of a cross-legged Hindu God, someone had carved a goatee. I wondered when this had happened, if it had been vandalized by the Buddhists who'd later taken over the temples from the Hindus, or if it was done by a tourist who'd forgotten themselves in a sacred place.

The land that cupped the temples had also once been heavy with landmines. In the distance, we saw the familiar red skull-and-crossbones signs that still warned of their presence. In the less-visited parts of the site, the signs bucked right up against narrow flights of stairs. If you tripped and fell over the side, you risked being blown apart.

Behind the temples, there was a landmine museum and an orphanage for children who'd survived their blasts. We paid our admission to a woman who explained that we would not see the children, it was not the orphanage's way. They were kids, not circus animals. Though the thought had never even occurred to us, we said nothing. There seemed no convincing way to deny it.

We were moving faster now, as if fleeing our own common sense that this thing between us would end. In Medan, Indonesia we found a city so devout that there were arrows pointing to Mecca in every room of our hotel. When I asked Noel about this, he said it was so you always knew which way to turn to face God.

I did not go into the streets of that city alone. The only time I had tried, a Jeep of men trailed slowly behind me in the sweating afternoon heat, shouting. It was, Noel explained, because I refused to cover my hair. In one of the malls, a woman detailed the folding of a headscarf to me, and even her fingers seemed patient, as if it was not my own stubbornness that had kept me from the garment, but simply that I hadn't known how to wear it. Sheepish, I did not correct her.

Hot and hungover, the muezzin call of the mosque next door woke us early each morning. Above me, the air-conditioner hummed, and an arrow reminded me I no longer prayed.

We spent our first afternoon at the Wildlife Museum, where we found no wildlife at all, but three floors of taxidermy. There were polar bears, two-headed sheep, cassowaries, and a dimly lit children's area stocked with baby animals. I spent the day peering into the mouths of kangaroos, wanting to stroke the tongues of hippopotamuses, and wondering at the neck and head of a giraffe, which had been propped in a flowerpot.

On our way back to the hotel, we found ourselves lost in the crush of bodies from a girls' school that had just let out for the day. They wanted pictures with our pale but unremarkable faces. I smiled as they took a hundred photos, pulling at the hem of my orange dress, holding the gauzy fabric against the stiff pleats of their own navy skirts.

Our days in that place were dwindling. Soon, we would have to get jobs and stop sleeping until noon, to sober up—though by the time I finally did we were no longer together.

But first, we left the early morning calls to prayer behind and headed south to a little town from which we hiked into the Sumatran jungle. There lay a still-active volcano, hot vapour spilling from cracks in the earth. Where the trees thickened, our guide led us to orangutans, the docile mothers cradling their children as they blinked curiously back at us with huge eyes. The males were more territorial, and much larger. An American man kept getting too close, wanting to take the perfect photo. The animal was huge. The shaggy red hair on its shoulders catching the sun as it ran at us.

In a clearing away from the threat of the American man, we sat down to eat lunch, the simple food seeming decadent after a hard climb over volcanic rock slicked with mud. A peacock wandered into the clearing to join us. We tossed scraps of our sandwiches to it as we marvelled at the liability that was its huge vibrant tail in the wild. The light was particularly beautiful then, the sun peeking through the canopy of trees in warm slats that I let fall across my upturned face.

Suddenly, I noticed a large man-shaped body emerging from the bush.

"Shit," I exclaimed, only loud enough to alert the guide to the orangutan in our midst, but not so loud the creature would startle.

We abandoned our meal and ran, tearing through the brush. It was a long way into the trees before we stopped, all of us panting, our hands on our knees. And when we looked at each other we could only laugh, the close call shredding our nerves like wire.

Closer to mine and Noel's bungalow, there were smaller monkeys. If you left your windows open, they would dart in and steal things. They seemed to like bars of soap the most. You would see the pilfered ivory rectangles dotting the rooftops of the local buildings. Whenever it rained, I expected to see bubbles coming down from the cluster of trees where the monkeys nestled among the branches, the cleanest simians in the whole world.

At last, we boarded a flight to my home country. On the twenty-some hours we spent in the air, I slept fitfully, sweating booze, and dreaming of endless markets, of helium balloons with illicit cargo, of tiny, unnamable animals, of mummified bodies in display cases, and of women who would never go home again.

A Steep Learning Curve

At the Sydney airport, I sat sipping a beer and waiting for my connecting flight to Melbourne, where I would live for the next year. The bartender was chatty, and the bar nearly empty.

"Did you know," she said, after glancing at my Canadian ID, "that here in Australia, I can serve a six-year-old a bourbon and coke with his meal if his guardian orders it for him?"

"Six?" I repeated dubiously. "And why bourbon?"

"It's just an example, the child could be any age," she said, and held the glass she was polishing up to the fluorescents overhead.

"You don't say."

"I do. Also, legal-aged husbands and wives can order for their underage spouses."

"Wild," I muttered. "You know, at sixteen, I'd have probably traded my freedom for a husband old enough to buy me wine coolers."

She grinned. "Then it's probably a good thing that you're not from around here."

I paid my bill and returned to the boarding area. I was still early and was surprised to find that among the flight codes for the delayed, boarding, and landed, there was one for my plane that I'd never seen before. It simply said: relax.

These first hints sparked an understanding of how far away from home I truly was. When I ducked into the washroom, the slogan on the Moxie products tampon dispenser advised me to, "Have a beautiful day in hell."

In Melbourne, I scrambled to decode Australian. I learned that in case of an emergency, I should call an Ambo, and if a man said my short skirt had made him crack a fat, I should slap him. A fanny is what my Canadian grandmother might call her ass. In Australia, it was popular slang for vagina. I learned the latter during a shopping trip with Netta, my then-boyfriend's mother. I was trying on pants and jokingly asked her, "Do these make my fanny look big?"

There was a long silence before she said, "I didn't really look dear."

When I first visited Netta, she had directed me down a hallway to the washroom. Once inside, I saw only a bathtub and sink. There was no toilet. I waffled over whether to pee in the sink or the tub, and what I would do later, when things became dire. I was just peering out the window to the back garden, and wondering when nightfall would come, when a knock sounded at the door.

"Are you okay in there dear?" Netta asked.

I peeked my head out and admitted, "I can't find the toilet."

Netta laughed for a long time before leading me to a little closet-sized room where the toilet stood alone. "We keep it separate down here," she explained. "It's more sterile I think."

On the flight in, I'd heard a few Australians ask for the toilet and had thought it shameless of them. Now I understood why they'd been so specific.

Not long into my stay, I drove up into the Dandenong Mountains to meet with a new friend I'd made at a writing group I'd joined. Further and further into the hills I rose, the huge ash trees whipping past my windows. The road switch-backed and seemed to disappear into the forest, the cars behind me honking as I made my way slowly in. Regardless of my careful driving, I still beat my friend to our meeting. She'd gotten hung up by hitting a postman with her car.

"He said it was the second time this month it'd happ ened to him," she told me fretfully.

"Jesus."

"He was really very calm about it. He seemed almost embarrassed, actually, as if it were his fault. But I think it's further proof that I really need a working speedometer in my car."

"Why don't you have a working speedometer?"

"Because it's an old car and an expensive fix. I don't have the cash right now, but I'm considering doing sex work of some kind to pay for it. Maybe BDSM. Something high-paying, but low-risk."

"Well, whatever you decide, I'm rooting for you."

"Pardon?"

"Rooting," I repeated, "you know, like I'm cheering for you."

"Ah," she said sagely, "in these parts, 'rooting' means fucking."

After lunch, she suggested we take the Puffing Billy Train even further into the hills. I agreed, and when the train arrived, we climbed on and I fell into the first available seat. My friend ignored this, and instead settled herself on the ledge where the window should have been. There were bars to hang onto, and several other riders followed suit.

"You're not really going to ride with your legs out the window, are you?" I asked.

"That's the whole point of this train," she explained, "to be scared shitless while the rainforest goes belting past you."

Tentatively, I slid in next to her, and the locomotive started up. As our legs dangled, the wind whipped at the hems of our dresses, and we had to hold them down while clinging on with our other hand. I could hardly remember a time I'd been so frightened. The trees I'd been afraid to drive into on the way up now seemed like they might reach out and snatch me from the ledge where I sat. My friend caught my eye as the train rounded a curve, throwing us back a little, so that we gripped the bars, our dresses shooting up as we let out giddy, identical screams.

That night, I still felt jazzed from the ride as I watched the news. An Australian politician's personal life had made headlines. He'd been caught sending out dick pics. In one, his penis dangled precariously over a glass filled to the rim with red wine. Back in Canada, one of our politicians had just been caught in a similar faux pas, but he hadn't thought to feature his member next to one of his country's chief exports. I suppose maple syrup just doesn't really have the same sex appeal as wine.

Feeling weirdly, yet familiarly inadequate, I moved to change the channel but was stopped cold by breaking news about the decade-long investigation into the murder of a local "Vampire Gigolo." I deflated into the couch. The murdered man had believed he needed to drink blood to live and had once bitten off a client's tongue.

"I feel woefully out of place," I complained a few days later to Bobby, another new friend.

"Relax," she said, echoing that flight code as if it had been a premonition. "Think about my situation. A ton of people in this country have seen me naked, and I could care less."

"I don't really see how that's the same as what I'm talking about," I said, for the sake of argument.

"My point is that you need to stop worrying about making mistakes."

"Maybe," I conceded.

"Come on," she pressed. "I'll show you the photos, so you can see what I don't allow to haunt me."

"I'd rather you didn't."

She ignored me and riffled through a closet until she found a stack of glossy magazines.

"See," she said, flipping to a centrefold. In the picture she was blonde, nude, and easily recognizable. "Things are only as big a deal as you make them out to be."

My prudish self never quite got over this admission, which is likely why I couldn't stop bringing it up afterwards.

"What do you think of these shoes?" she would ask.

"Oh, they're really you," I'd gush. "And I'd know. I've seen your vagina."

She ignored my fumbling and continued to prepare for her wedding that summer. When she ceased asking for my opinions, I didn't blame her. Nor did I fault her fiancé for avoiding my bumbling self at parties. I never did master the swift, dry, double kiss greeting that is the Australian norm. I was prone to nerves and panting, and this led me to sometimes get people, quite wetly, in the ear. I'd see Bobby's fiancé fleeing from me, just after I'd caught his eye and had begun to move towards him. He'd exit out the front door without his shoes, or close himself in the bathroom—as I heard the surprised cries of the person already inside who'd forgotten to lock themselves in.

When I was introduced to my boyfriend's aunt, a woman who was nearly blind, I'd somehow kissed her on the mouth. She graciously pretended it was nothing out of the ordinary.

"Canada, you say. What's that like at this time of year?" I heard her utter to the space where I'd been standing. For I had fled and was already halfway across the room.

I kept mostly to the sprawling southeastern suburbs of Melbourne. But, on a rare day in the city centre, I emerged from Flinders Street Station in time to spot a passing judge, his black robes billowing in the wind. I watched, agog, as he clasped a hand atop the enormous, curling white wig that belonged to a former century. Then, he ran against the light and into a sandwich shop.

His was a feat that I would never master. I was nearly run over every time I tried to cross the street. When I'd asked Netta what I was doing wrong, she'd scolded me. "You have to cross at the zebra crossings."

"But I am," I insisted.

I could tell from her expression that she didn't believe me. Perhaps she thought we didn't even have stripes in Canada, only lots and lots of plaid. My new roommate Fred—who was an old friend of my then-boyfriend—wasn't sympathetic either.

"You'll figure it out," Fred told me with a shrug, "or you'll be killed."

He had the same attitude towards my driving, which was a nervous thing to watch as I told myself repeatedly to drive on the lefthand side. Sydney had signs to remind drivers of this, but in Melbourne you were on your own. I threaded through residential neighbourhoods and tried to rewire my brain. I also received my first speeding ticket, though Fred had some advice for how best to deal with that.

"Just write a letter apologizing," he advised. "Tell them you're Canadian and that you don't know any better."

I'd scoffed at the suggestion but gave it a try. Sure enough, the fine was waived. Though next time, the Victoria Police assured me, I wouldn't be let off the hook so easily.

Fred was a serious hoarder. In the rear living room, there were the remains of his model plane habit, and in the one at the front of the house, he had editions of the local paper, some dating back to the previous decade.

"Think of it as a library," he instructed, as he shifted a pile of vintage porn off the couch and onto the floor so I could sit down. "If you have any questions about things that have happened in this suburb, you'll be able to find an answer here."

When he moved an American football helmet aside, it dislodged a large Huntsman spider that had been tucked snuggly inside. It stretched, expanding to the size of a housecat, and disappeared into the detritus. More critters started turning up: one spider with a little white spot on the tip of its abdomen, and then another just like it, which suggested a nest somewhere.

"Don't touch those," Fred advised.

"I wasn't planning on it."

"I mean it. They're White Tails, they can give you a terrible sort of festering rash. It can even flare up years afterwards."

I shrank back and asked, "Do you know what a White Tail is in Canada?"

Fred shook his head.

"It's a type of deer. Like Bambi."

"Just try to be more careful," Fred cautioned. "Shake the bedsheets out before you bring them inside from the clothesline. White Tails love to hide in linens."

"Of course they do," I muttered.

As a rule, I avoided our backyard. The lawn was wildly overgrown. Fred had put in a post for the hop plants to climb up in the rear corner and, when they overtook it, a crossbeam.

"It's the house with the giant cross in the backyard," I told new friends. "You can spot it from blocks away. Stop by any time."

But they never did.

The lawn's overgrowth harboured snakes. I took to tottering out to the clothesline in knee-high platform boots, paired with a one-piece bathing suit because of the oppressive heat. I'd see the neighbours' curtains flutter and narrate the scene behind them in my head: a middle-aged man waving his wife over as yelled, "Margery, come quick. The dominatrix is at it again."

On one such occasion, Fred came out to show me the latest edition of the local paper. A nonagenarian woman in Queensland had been beaten up by a kangaroo while bringing in her washing. The police were called, but the animal refused to vacate her yard, so the officers had to pepper spray it.

"See," Fred intoned, "this sort of thing is why you need to be cautious."

"I am cautious," I huffed, gesticulating to my boots.

"Have you heard of Drop Bears?" he asked, as if he hadn't heard me. "They're similar to koalas, only bigger and carnivorous. They drop out of trees and onto their unsuspect ing prey, which sometimes includes people."

"You're kidding."

"They're especially drawn to the lily-white skin of Englishmen."

"Oh, fuck off. This country's so crazy, you don't need to make up fake scary animals."

I stormed off, leaving him to collect the last of the linens. Though I was forced to let my demeanor thaw only a few days later, when I called Fred from the safety of my car.

"Yes?" he answered, pushing aside the curtains to see that I was parked out front.

I pointed to the large Huntsman spider on my driver's side door. Intent on getting inside, it had already worked two of its legs through the crack in the top of the window. What's more, I'd spotted it on my car that morning and had driven some 200 kilometres with it clinging on. Fred came out and killed the spider without even putting on shoes, sacrificing the latest issue of the *Berwick Star News* for the cause.

I called my boyfriend that night and told him what had happened. He was working away at the time, in some part of Australia unknown to me. But even over the crackling of our poor connection, I could hear the judgement in his voice. "I don't see what the big deal is. They just like to crawl into cars sometimes to have their babies."

By then, we were already on the outs. But given my pending status as his sponsor to Canada, I felt I was in too deep. Soon after he returned to Melbourne for a short visit, a spider took up residence on the ceiling over our bed. It had an abdomen of shocking turquoise, a colour that, if not a marker for something poisonous, was certainly trying to mimic that attribute. I worried about it dropping into my open mouth while I slept.

This was nonsense, my boyfriend declared. He'd noticed the spider days before, and it hadn't moved since. It was, according to him, "certainly dead." Days passed. Finally, I convinced him to deal with the spider. "Would you look at that," he quipped admiringly, while shuffling it into a drinking glass, "it's still alive."

Despite my misgivings, we flew out to Brisbane soon afterward, where we spent a handful of sunny days fighting on patios. We headed north to Cairns, where we lolled about on the beaches, the saltwater smell thick in the air.

I saw a sign for a Cthulhu-like creature, pointed it out and asked, “What’s that?”

“It’s a jellyfish,” my partner explained, and lifted a jewel-toned bottle of something from a little hutch beneath the sign. “This vinegar helps to neutralize the venom from the sting.”

“Why is the vinegar blue?”

“So people won’t use it on their fish-and-chips.”

A few days later, we found ourselves on a beach deep in the Daintree Rainforest, loaded with warning signs for crocodiles. I stayed away from the shore, watching as strangers allowed their babies and poodles to play in the surf. My boyfriend pulled me away from the spectacle to a little pond where he coaxed me to squat down.

“Do you know what this is?” he asked.

I shook my head and leaned a little closer to the water.

He pointed to a marker. “This is where a crocodile came up and bit a guy in the face. He lived though.”

I shot backwards, scrabbling across the sand on my butt. “Why do you hate me so much?” I asked.

“Relax,” he said, echoing a word I was, by now, quite sick of. He gestured towards the ocean, and to two girls bobbing quite a distance away from the beach. They were screaming with laughter. “If anyone’s getting eaten, it’s those two.”

I said nothing but thought of the car with the blown head gasket he’d purchased for me, and the job at the café in the middle of nowhere he'd helped me to secure through a friend. The girls at the café referred to me as "the girl from Woop Woop," meaning far away. When I'd balked about driving into an unpopulated stretch of nothing in such an unreliable vehicle, he'd filled my trunk with water and insisted that I would be just fine. The message was clear: I would either live, or I wouldn't.

As if to sweat me right out of the country, the temperatures climbed during my last months in Melbourne. A news anchorwoman spoke of car dashboards melting in the heat. One forty-degree day bled into a string of ten, and the air-conditioning at work gave out. I made blended drinks and dumped the left-over crushed ice straight down my top, the floor growing slick around my feet. I fielded calls from customers about the indoor temperature and whether we had a cool, private space for women to breastfeed. When I relayed this latter point to a fellow employee, she'd suggested that new mothers feed their infants in their cars.

"They'd curdle," I'd said, and then had to explain what that meant.

I stopped caring that my body looked like a lumpy bag of mashed potatoes after months of hard drinking. I lived in bathing suits. I'd fill my top with whatever cool produce was in the refrigerator and wander around like a glorified fruit bowl.

"Those are my capsicums," Fred told me one afternoon, gesturing to the red peppers that were heating up against my breasts.

"So," I said, shrugging a little and nearly losing one of them.

"So, you're a shit housemate."

"Yeah," I replied, grinning, "so are you."

I was working three jobs by then, one at an electronics store. On yet another unbearably hot afternoon, we found shit on the floor of the shop. We all thought the culprit was the seeing eye dog guiding a blind man earlier in the day. But then we watched the camera footage.

An elderly woman in billowy slacks shuffled through the aisles. She paused at one of the shelves, as if to inspect a digital camera. Then, suddenly, she began to shake something out of her pantleg. When she'd finished with the task, she strode off, her eyes fixed straight ahead on the world in front of her.

She was a woman afraid of nothing. Not the language, not the spiders, not the heat. She did not even have to ask where the toilet was. She would make her own.

Reasons to Live

I went to Bratislava because I was tired of being owned by other people, of being violated by them. There was the man on a Thai island who'd waited until the porchlight switched off outside my bungalow before stepping out of the shadows. There was the boy who'd helped himself to my body when we were on a date. There were girlfriends, people I loved like sisters, who'd attempted to give me to their partners without my consent. Once, as a Christmas present.

After a particularly bad long-term relationship ended, I had attempted to level the field by dating indiscriminately. I saw two or three men at a time. I called them by nicknames until they blurred into one person: the Man in Apartment 211, the Racist, the Pilot, the Vegan, the Guy with the Tail, and Mr. November. I would follow them home with little more reason than curiosity about what their residences looked like. The next morning, trying to find the bathroom, I'd take a wrong turn, and end up in a closet or the garage. Once I stumbled on a deer corpse suspended from the ceiling. On another occasion, I was startled to find that the man I'd gone home with collected masks—or worse—that perhaps his mother did.

I was intent on my own destruction. I walked through the woods alone at night with packs of coyotes on the edges of the path. I drank to excess and then recuperated in the rooms of strangers. I got into the habit of leaving something of mine behind, of closing a sock into a cutlery drawer before walking out with one shoe sliding around on my bare foot. It was akin to scrawling my initials on the wall of a bathroom stall.

I assumed it was my slutty bravado that attracted these people initially. I thought if I showcased myself as being from the sample tray, left out for long enough under the florescent grocery store lights, anyone who was even possibly interested in me would eventually see the greasy sheen of my left-behind-self and move along.

It's not that I had explicit plans to kill myself or that I'd even mapped out how I would do it, but I was then trying to come up with reasons to live. Walling myself up in Slovakia, in a city where no one spoke my language, where tourists were few and far between and where most people living there would leave if they could, seemed like a way to test myself.

After I'd finished packing up my apartment, I went to see my previous partner to drop off the last of his things. I stood in the entryway of his apartment saying my goodbyes when he grabbed both of my wrists. When I tried to pull away, he attempted to kiss me anyway. I had to struggle to get away from him and after I managed to, I ran out into the hallway.

He called after me, "If you won't sleep with me, why do I even have a bed?"

By the looks of things, I didn't even deserve to be asked for consent anymore. I felt so tired of myself and of my body.

Before I left Canada, I saw one of the men I'd been dating. We hung out in my airless apartment and talked. He had invited himself over though I had made it clear I wasn't really in any shape for company. Still, he came and played me a few songs on the guitar that sat in my living room among the boxes.

When I was younger, I would let people do the things they wanted, because it meant that afterwards they would leave. But I refused to do that now.

"I'm tired of being touched," I confided when he placed a hand of my knee. We both knew he'd come over expecting something physical, and yet I was charmed when he just asked if he could hold me and then did. I cried myself out on the floor's stiff carpet and he left only when I was finished.

I spent the two weeks before I went to Bratislava with a good friend in Stockholm, taking as much rock crystal MDMA as I could (a drug I quickly discovered will dig a you-shaped pit beneath your feet if you're prone to depression) and switching to pills when that ran out, asking what I'd just taken only after I'd already swallowed it. My friend and I went to museums and watched movies. We took speed and I felt more trapped in my own body than I ever had. We wandered the city and drank wine together on a nearby archipelago.

One afternoon, he took me on a sort of suicide tour. "You're twice as likely to kill yourself in Sweden as you are to die in a car accident," he told me.

It was late afternoon, and we stood on a cliff overlooking some train tracks. There were white canvas shoes on the edge. The shoes were still new, as if they'd just been purchased, walked to this spot, and stepped out of—the wearer's decision as sudden and unexpected as a muscle spasm.

I didn't tell my friend what I was thinking I might do, though he'd looked at me incredulously and asked, "Bratislava? Why the fuck would you want to go there?"

Before I left Stockholm, I rented an apartment in Bratislava through a website. The woman subletting it to me was confused. "You want my place for a month? I mean, are you sure? Most people only stay a few days." Even she had moved to Spain because, she informed me, she loved to dance.

Though I had resolved to go to Bratislava, I couldn't help but be a little afraid of yet another new city. I had been assaulted multiple times while traveling, sometimes in the most unlikely of places.

Once, I had even been grabbed while praying in a temple in Laos. This was in a city that had appeared entirely holy in the mornings—the parade of hundreds of monks making their way through the streets to collect alms. The orange tide of their robes poured over me like the waters of a baptism. After seeing the procession, I felt like praying. But the only other person with me inside the sacred space had reached out to stroke the tattoo on my foot and when I had looked up in surprise at his touch, he had grasped my instep and dragged me towards him on the tile floor. I had felt the ridges of the tiles through the fabric of my cotton dress as they slid past. We were alone there, and I knew no one was coming.

In an earlier version of this story, I claimed to have kicked out at him. But this wasn't true. I froze. When his grip slackened, I wrenched away and ran. I was so ashamed of my own fear and confused that sometimes I was strong and sometimes I was not, I could not even confess to it on the page.

Bratislava did turn out to be desolate, even more so than I had imagined. I was used to the often-predictable kindness of Canadian strangers, so when I couldn't find my apartment, it was hard to locate someone who'd even look at the map I had, much less loan me their phone so I could call the woman who was waiting for me somewhere nearby.

Most of my days were spent being yelled at in a language I couldn't understand. I'd tried to learn the basics. Like Alexander Graham Bell on the first telephone call, the citizens of Bratislava said "ahoy" instead of hello, but much beyond that I got lost. I was yelled at by old women outside churches, by bus drivers when they'd reached the end of their routes and wanted me off, by security guards at grocery stores when I mistakenly exited out the entrance. I wondered if this was a symptom of communism, if its coldness had settled into the bones of the city and stayed there.

Even my rented apartment appeared not to want me. Changing the sheets, I accidentally stuck my fingers into an open electrical socket behind the bed and received a shock I felt in my right hand for days. I got stuck in the elevator. And, after the main light in the apartment burned out, I spent days in the dark, trading out the lightbulb many times before finally calling my landlord's father. He turned out to be an electrician and wanted to know why I hadn't called him sooner.

When, in a little bar a short walk from my place, I came upon a bartender who spoke a handful of English words and had family in Ontario, I nearly climbed over the bar to hug him. There was something about the men of the place. I liked their brusqueness. I'm sure it was only the way it came across to me, but it seemed like they were always yelling at their wives and girlfriends. Yet somehow, they also behaved like gentlemen. Holding open the door for their partner while they yelled, carrying her oversized purse while they yelled, and helping her on with her coat as they screamed at the back of her head.

"I have an oversized purse," I wanted to say, "I have a coat. Look, that door needs opening." I was so starved for contact by then that their brusqueness looked like romance to me, and I was trying to distract myself from the thing that I had come to do. Though I eventually became grateful for this perceived invisibility, for the way I could move through the crowds without a second look by the men. It was safer.

Years before, alone on a beach in Vietnam, I had been playing in the surf. The cold water licked at the hem of my dress as I waded into the ocean. When it was above my knees, my dress ballooned around me where the waves caught it. At this moment, I turned to see a man on the bluff above, watching me and masturbating. I stared at him for a moment, afraid, because it was only the two of us on that beach. And then I raised my tiny waterproof camera to one eye and watched as he stumbled away, his pants still too far down for him to properly mount his motorcycle as he skidded up onto the highway and out of sight.

In Bratislava, I couldn't blame the locals for their indiff erence to me. The country suffered greatly from brain drain. There were better jobs to be had elsewhere, and once citizens were educated, they left. So, what was I doing here, exploring a place that everyone seemed all too keen to run from?

On a walking tour through the city, I followed a young guide who'd been born in 1993, the same year the Czech Republic separated. She told us that when the movie *Hostel* came out (a horror movie supposedly set in Bratislava, but actually filmed somewhere in Prague), tourism went down seventy-five percent, as if the industry was just such a precarious thing.

The guide, whose name I have forgotten, took us to the blue church, a huge building that was created in Art Nouveau style. It looked as if it were built from plasticine. "Some people call it the Smurf Church," she recounted. "My grandparents were married there, most people from the city are married in it, and I assume I will be one day too."

She pointed across the street to an asylum that had been abandoned about a decade before. The city owned it, and it was supposed to be torn down, but still it stood. The asylum had horrific, ghoulish sculptures of tortured humans on it, their mouths open in screams. "I can't directly translate what it says on the door," she said, "but it's something along the lines of, 'if you enter here, you will not leave.'"

How odd it seemed to me then, on what was supposed to be the happiest day of your life, to walk out the front doors of the church and see that.

In Bratislava, I felt safer than I had in many other cities and towns. Still, I was careful to be home by dusk. The one night that I'd been out after dark, a group of three men surrounded me in front of the bar nearest my apartment. I didn't know what they were saying, but I knew what came next. They advanced, and I stood still. But just then an elderly woman came out of the bar, cane in hand, and began to yell at them. They scattered like so much smoke. I turned to thank her, and she began her verbal assault on me. I didn't know what she was saying, but I had the sense that it was a question of what I was doing out alone at this hour. Sheepishly, I fled too.

I felt that the trouble with having so many things happen to you, is that you begin to feel like you're somehow responsible. Some years after Bratislava, when I summed up the mountain of these occurrences to a friend, he had suggested, in a voice that I'm sure was intended to be gentle, "Perhaps it's the way you present yourself that suggests to them that you're asking for it."

To spend more time outside of my Bratislava apartment, I developed a running obsession. I say obsession because at two in the afternoon, sometime after it'd hit 30°C, I would run, and I would try to do this every day. I liked to go to the sparsely populated path around the river. There were only ever a handful of people out walking their dogs and staring at me as I went past, sure that they would get to watch my death from heat exhaustion if they just kept their eyes on me. After one particularly hot run I returned to my apartment dizzy and confused. I went to bed and slept until the next morning, still feeling sick when I woke, but better. After that I took to running in the early evening.

It was on these later outings that I met the man who might've saved me. He had Down syndrome, and perhaps it was the thing that made him like no one else, the openness on his face like nothing I'd seen in that city. He too ran in the evenings and when I saw him, his face lit up and he would high-five me as I passed. It was the only physical contact I had for an entire month, and by the end of that time I loved him like a soulmate.

In that lonely city, I wasn't eating much. It takes a certain kind of bravery to eat in restaurants alone, and I didn't have that then. Nor did I know how to explain that I was a vegetarian, though I'd practiced saying the Slovak word many times. So, I cooked alone in my little apartment. I bought soup packs for one: a shrink-wrapped carrot, a potato, an odd root vegetable, a sprig of parsley, and a single clove of garlic. I wrestled with the tiny oven and the burners of the stovetop. I hadn't realized that you had to flip the thing open, and so, the first time I'd lit one of the burners, a great ball of flame came shooting out at me. I was squatting down at the time and lost most of my eyebrows and all but the top inch of my bangs.

I came to discover that in Bratislava, what you were going to have for dinner depended on what you could find at the grocery store. Yesterday, there might've been mountains of tomatoes but today, when you wanted to concoct homemade salsa, there were none. Or, you'd decided upon mushroom soup, and now there was only one sad cremini half-flattened on the floor, wearing the tread of someone's shoe.

I learned to improvise, to throw in handfuls of lentils and watch as my soup came out the other side as a stew and my casseroles became watery, odd things. I drank lots and lots of coffee while I waited to see what I had made, sweeping around my dark apartment in a half-run, my blood espresso-thick and my heart like a hummingbird in my chest.

I thought I was getting better. But it was perhaps more like those stories you read with some level of horror as the main character becomes more ill and yet is sure they're filling their bodies with light they've eaten while laying on their beds in what only they can see as a perfect right angle to the face of God.

Still, over the course of the month I was there, I fell for Bratislava in a way I couldn't explain. I loved the blue bathtub, its porcelain the same inexplicable shade of blue as my hair. I loved going to sleep to the sound of the bar near my apartment, with its strange music—a blend of polka and electronica, like nothing I'd ever heard and haven't since. I loved the screenless window of my third-floor apartment, and the way, when I dangled my lower body out of the window the hot night wrapped itself around my legs like a blanket. When I'd first arrived, I thought about tumbling out of that window all the time, but worried that with only three stories to fall, it would not do the kind of damage I was looking for.

I walked more. I explored the neighbourhood and vast walking paths, the desolate graffiti that marred buildings and bridges. The one English phrase I found said only, "I'm too old for this shit." I took photos of torn-up benches and groups of people rolling enormous tires. I listened to podcast after podcast: my daily feast of English. Ira Glass' voice in my ear like its own melody. He was one of the handful of things that carried me through that time, and I feel a deep love for him still.

One evening near the end of my time there, I wandered to my usual running path and came face-to-face with an elephant. I'd heard a sort of strange bleating the night before, and as I stood in front of the huge grey creature, it occurred to me just what the noise had been. It turned out a circus was travelling through, and they'd settled their animals in makeshift pens near the banks of the Danube, still inside the borders of the city. The backdrop of buildings behind the elephant's vast head seeming so incongruent and strange.

By the end of the month, I couldn't imagine leaving. I took photos of my communist bloc apartment building. But now, when I look at those pictures of rows of buildings all the same, I can't totally be sure which one was mine.

At the train station, I bought a one-way ticket to Budapest. The woman at the desk informed me that it was only a single Euro to return to Bratislava, though it was sixteen to get all the way to Budapest. I thought about coming back, but it seemed to me that I had to leave the city behind. That for me, it had done all it could.

Alone in the Kitchen with a Zebra

When I first thought to visit Paris, I was living in Edmonton, a city with a little over one-hundred people per square kilometre. Paris had more than twenty thousand populating that same area. The idea of a place where so many people lived on top of each other seemed a dystopian nightmare to me. Solitude was an easy thing to find at home. Skyscrapers backed onto river valley trails and coyotes strolled through suburbs at the pace of someone popping out to get the mail. I'd grown up in a small town and found it reassuring on sleepless nights to wander out into the woods near my home and stumble on a four-point buck, the creature staring just as curiously back at me.

Elise met me at the Gare du Nord train station. Despite the rush of strangers, I spotted her easily among the crowd.

It was her grin that gave her away, and the huge wool sweater patterned with reindeer. A fellow Canadian, Elise had been living in the city for some time now, working as a language tutor and au pair. The latter paid both in cash and the use of a twelve-square-metre apartment in the sixth arrondissement.

"My place is really tiny," she confided, as she crushed me into a hug, "but you're welcome to stay as long as you like."

I clung to the strap of her bag as we hustled through the crowds and into the Métro. On the platform we were nearly separated by the steady rush of strangers. Elise had to grab my hand and yank me up onto the train, exclaiming, "I've never seen it quite like this."

Inside the train, we found a somewhat solitary corner, where I set my backpack atop my feet so it would take up less room.

"You know," Elise said thoughtfully, "I used the Métro to move. Can you imagine that? You're fighting through the same crowds; except you're carrying all your worldly possessions."

And I said that I could not.

Once inside her building, I followed Elise up four winding flights of stairs. I reached for the railing once when I lost my footing, and it wobbled in my grip with all the integrity of dental floss.

"Keep in mind that drinking requires planning," she advised. "I've found you can't get too soused and climb these stairs."

"Right," I agreed, puffing after her.

The cramped entryway of the apartment—where Elise stored most of her belongings—took up the lion's share of the space. In the heart of it, there was room for a slender single bed and the desk that would double as our dining table. Two mattresses were stacked atop the bedframe, one of which would later be laid out on the floor so we could both sleep at the same time.

"I'll sit on the bed during meals," Elise explained, "because there's only enough space for one chair."

The set-up reminded me of Laurie Colwin's essay, "Alone in the Kitchen with an Eggplant," in which the author cooks strange meals with her lone pot inside "an apartment the size of a place mat." Elise seemed to have worked out how best to live in the small space, though I doubted she'd have been able to host a dinner party for four the way Colwin had. Nor was there a bathtub to do the dishes in afterwards.

"It's tiny," Elise repeated, as she slid my backpack beneath the bed and out of the way, "but you can't beat the location or the view."

The window opened out onto the massive scaffold of the Eiffel Tower, its metal bones reaching up into the deepening black of the sky. I lit a cigarillo and puffed into the breeze. It was late now, and the lights of the tower flashed once more before shutting off for the night.

The next morning, I woke up with a red wine hangover. I sat up in the bed Elise had ceded to me and poured a glass of water from the kitchen sink. I limped to the bathroom, where posters from French movie houses covered the holes in the walls. Outside the door, Elise turned up the radio loud enough to give me the false sense of privacy. After we'd dressed, she led me to a nearby park where we ran sloppily past statues older than our home country, our heads pounding.

"This is my usual circuit," Elise explained, as we dragged ourselves, lungs burning, through the crisp Parisian fall air. A woman in a long, sleek coat came up beside us. She paused just long enough to crush out her cigarette with the pointed toe of her tasteful flat, before passing us as if we were standing still.

Elise and I had met a few years before, in a shabby bar where I'd worked for nearly a decade, and where she'd been given her first waitressing gig. The bar stood in the neighbourhood of that coyote-filled city where Elise had also grown up—the stuccoed houses of which were riddled with holes made by the local woodpeckers.

A few weeks before Christmas, Elise had lost her footing on the slick walkway in front of the bar. She'd gone down quickly, too quick even to put her hands out, and had broken her two front teeth. When she peeled back her bloody lips to show those of us on shift, two jagged stumps remained. One regular who worked as a nurse had swivelled around on his stool and peered into the cavern of Elise's mouth. "The damage," he slurred, "is catastrophic."

As an actress working in local productions, Elise had more reasons than most to worry. Dentist after dentist gave her dizzying estimates about the cost of fixing her central incisors. As luck would have it, she landed a winter role traveling with a children's production. The kids identified with her through the gaps in their smiles and the singing of "All I Want for Christmas is my Two Front Teeth." After the show's run ended, she found a dentist who discovered all her nerves were still intact and successfully capped the broken teeth.

Later, she'd parlayed the experience into a play. On a projection screen, the audience watched a young woman making snow angels on a lake, her grin proudly displaying its busted front teeth in the footage Elise's sister had thought to capture.

When Elise decided to leave Edmonton in favour of Paris, I'd balked. Not only would I miss her, but I also couldn't fathom her desire to live in what I imagined to be a chaotic place. In my hometown of seven-thousand people, my favorite pastime had been driving what remained of my cloud-blue, beat-up Toyota out to the narrow oilfield roads threading around the townsite. On those afternoons, I often wouldn't see a soul, and the only sound I'd hear was the pinging of gravel hitting my wheel wells.

After our run, Elise and I took turns stretching—as there wasn't room for both of us on the floor. Before leaving for a tutoring appointment, she'd mapped the transfers I had to take to visit the Louvre. In the Métro, people hustled in swarms. Teenagers on skateboards headed straight for me, only to swerve at the last moment, as if playing a game of chicken I was unaware of.

At a food truck parked just beyond the museum's glass pyramids, I joined a small line-up. When I was just about to order, a woman stepped in front of me, her hair filling my mouth she was so close. She ordered the last of the item I wanted, and I reached for the foulest word I knew and spit it into her coif. Later, Elise would assure me that the woman had understood. The word was nearly the same in English and French.

Inside the Louvre, I was surprised to find huge escal ators ferrying museumgoers between floors. Large rooms spooled off into warrens of smaller ones, and I understood why someone might want a weeklong pass to the place. I flitted through, unsure of where I was headed.

I paused to gape at the detail of Vermeer's *The Lacemaker* and a statue of Psyche reaching up to embrace Cupid. But my reverence dissolved when I found myself abruptly swept up in a crush of people. They were, I gleaned from the conversations of the strangers around me, on their way to see the Mona Lisa. In the distance, I spotted the tiny, gilded frame, and the dark-haired woman captured inside of it. This fleeting sight was enough for me.

I scooted diagonally through the stream and towards a set of stairs. Several other strangers had the same idea, and together we hustled away. We moved at a steady clip until the woman directly in front of me stopped abruptly, and I nearly fell over backwards to avoid colliding with her.

"Dear God," I exclaimed.

The man at my side, who darted successfully from one near catastrophe to the next advised, "Just brush it off and keep moving. Don't ever stop." He was dragging a woman with him through the throng of bodies. Her face had the look of someone who'd been grabbed by mistake but thought her situation preferable to being left behind.

Soon, we were shepherded into a room along with another hundred or so people. I looked up at the vast painted frescos on the ceiling and back down again just in time to see the museum guards shut the door behind us and lock it. The people around me chatted nervously, trying to figure out what was going on. We grew restless at our confinement, the minutes spooling by as we shook the locked doors until someone came to let us out without explanation.

Rattled, I stepped onto an escalator that hurtled to the basement to the museum's collection of lesser-known statuary. It was dark down there, and cool. In painted marble, the carefully chiseled face of Isis stared back at me from an earlier century. I stood in front of her, my heart slowing. Grateful that it was only us in the space.

The next morning, Elise and I sat sipping espresso, fresh from the heat of her single-burner hotplate. I glanced up to see her fix me with a grave look. I thought she was going to tell me that she'd been wrong, that her quarters were in fact too tight to house the both of us. Instead, she announced, "You're welcome to go by yourself, but I will not be visiting Versailles for the umpteenth time. There's always so many people there that you can hardly move."

I thought of the day before. Of the closeness of strangers. On the ride home, I'd fished an alien blonde hair from my mouth. "Well, why would I want to go then?" I asked.

"Because everybody goes."

"Not everybody."

Hoping it would prove slightly less hectic, we headed to the city's catacombs. Alas, a line snaked out from beneath the subterranean expanse of the city. We were not the only ones wanting to see the stacks of bones that lined the walls beneath our feet.

"What do you think?" Elise asked, as we took in the serpentine cluster of strangers.

"I think I should have peed before we left your place."

"Always."

Soon, those of us in line were split up into groups. The space we were waiting to enter was narrow. Only so many of us would be let in at a time.

In the damp coolness, the remains of the city's former citizens were stacked on top of each other. Some of the bones were even arranged in recognizable shapes. Skulls were piled into crosses and curved into hearts. Elise translated the plaques and writings for me, while those who treaded alongside us shrieked when they got too close to the remains. Slowly, the walkways began to curve back up towards the surface. On our exit, those with large handbags were stopped and searched.

"What could they possibly take?" I asked Elise.

"Sometimes people make off with bones," she replied, taking my hand and pulling me the last of the way, up into the glare of the city sunlight. Out in that brightness, we found our bodies coated with a layer of white dust. I wondered if, in this accidental way, we too had made off with something that did not belong to us.

Elise and I dipped down into the Métro once more and boarded a train, where the exits were quickly blocked off with people. I'd begun to panic a little each time this happened, and Elise developed a game to distract me from this anxiety. She began to read all the very French-sounding stops in her most terrible Anglo-Saxon English accent. By the time *saynt duh-nee* became Saint Dennis, I'd dissolved into giggles on the hard metro seats we'd somehow procured amid the chaos.

There was one last classic tourist thing I wanted to do while in Paris. I wished to visit the Eiffel Tower grounds, if only to fathom the size of the structure. But, Elise hedged, we would do it her way. This, it turned out, meant that we did not get any closer than the half-a-dozen couples who wanted the tower backdropped in their wedding photos. We watched from the roadside, as the wide, white tulle bells of the brides' dresses brushed dangerously close to the grilles of the honking cars passing by.

"Enough?" Elise asked me, after we'd passed three-quarters of an hour this way. I nodded, and she swept me into the opposite direction of the milling crowds. We jumped on the Métro a few stations down the line, not wanting to join those fresh with frustration from the ongoing shoving match beneath the tower.

With this done, I found myself recalling the words of a man in Budapest I'd rented an apartment from. In a review, he'd said I wasn't the usual tourist. Perhaps because I'd once asked him for directions to a small medical museum containing the city's first pair of forceps.

In Paris, I set aside the must-see lists of others and spent an afternoon at the Deyrolle taxidermy museum. While there, a stuffed animatronic hog opened its mouth to greet Elise and me with a French song. We strolled through room after room of posed beasts. Most were available for rent. I thought of that impossible dinner party in Elise's apartment, and just where we might put a stuffed zebra. Though when I looked over at her face, in quiet concentration over the regal form of a seated lion, I knew the subject was already closed.

Across the Seine at the Museum of Hunting and Nature, the taxidermy was more obscene. In one room, poker-playing chimps sat around a table. In another, an elk had a red gown draped over its antlers. It was the latter tableau that clued me in to my homesickness. I'd been away from Canada for three months by then. I thought of my friends back home whose husbands still coveted the wild and the stuffed. One had made the best of it, using the outstretched horns of a mounted moose to dry her bras. She sometimes forgot about them, and I'd come in to see pink, lacy cups brushing the creature's nose, as if I'd caught it in the act of huffing her lingerie.

Elise and I returned to the apartment in the sixth arrondissement with wine in tow.

"Paris is a city with so many museums that if you visited one every day for a year, you would not see them all. And this is what you choose," she marveled.

"Without regret," I said, grinning as I clinked my glass against hers. We sat next to each other on her narrow single bed, waiting for the lights of the tower we'd seen almost-up-close to go out.

The following day, Elise escorted me to the Père Lachaise cemetery and left me alone in the sprawling necropolis. I'd expected crowds, but found I had the cobblestone pathways mostly to myself. I hovered before Jim Morrison's grave, my shadow solitary over his tombstone. A fence had been erected around the grave, and hundreds of ribbons and bracelets dangled from it, moving soundlessly in the breeze. I felt as if I'd just missed those scores of mourners.

It was the same at Oscar Wilde's grave, where a glass case covered the tombstone. Lip prints in every possible shade marked the glass—as if nothing would impede Wilde's admirers' devotion.

It seemed I was finally starting to settle into the city. And because Elise kept telling me I could stay as long as I liked, I began to think about changing my flight home to a later date. Ours was an easy companionship, even when packed-in so tightly together. That bar back in Canada, with its thimble-sized kitchen, had surely prepared us for this. Once upon a time, we had to contort our bodies like dancers carrying steaming plates of food, as we did everything that we could not to burn one another. Now we had only to mind the points of each others' elbows as I darted behind Elise at the sink, and into her little bathroom.

There was a concert I wanted to attend eight days after I was to leave Paris. A month or so before, while visiting a restaurant on the outskirts of Budapest, I'd been able to see into the kitchen as I sat at the bar counter. Two men stood on the line sautéing eggplant and scream-singing to each other lyrics from "I Gotta Feelin (Just Nineteen)."

As one of the men slid my meal across the counter, he told me about the show they would be attending in Paris. "We're going to take the train in the night before," he said. "It sounds like a good enough reason to visit the city."

At the time, I had been trying not to plan too far ahead, unsure if I'd be alive for the days on the horizon. But I had begun to notice a lifting in myself and in the sky—not that it was so remarkable in Paris. It was close to winter then, the clouds the grey of an overcoat. But the fact I'd noticed them at all was something, as if all that space had suddenly opened up overhead.

In the quiet of the cemetery, I hummed the song and stepped carefully between the rows of graves, considering what it might be like to stay just a little longer and how funny it would be to run into those singing men.

On one of Elise's free afternoons, she and I headed to the Paleontology Museum. The museum was in an area with many others, and I saw how easy it would be to spend the days going from one to the next. The buildings with their hundreds of windows imprinted themselves on my dreams and that night I walked through corridors of glass.

Inside the museum, Elise and I peered into jars with pickled cyclopic cats and twin sheep embryos that had fused together. As we'd hoped, there were few enough people in attendance that we could move easily between exhibits. In the quiet rooms belonging to drawers filled with small fossils, there was no one but us.

In the main hall, I peered up into the skeleton of a narwhal, a creature I had believed, up until that moment, to be extinct.

"They're still out there," Elise assured me, as our eyes followed the trajectory of its single huge canine. The tooth pointed skyward, to a ceiling festooned with the ribcage staves of elephant bones, which looked every bit like a prehistoric children's mobile. We stayed until we were dizzy with hunger, our growling bellies echoing in the quiet.

We had planned to picnic somewhere for lunch, and Elise insisted on making a stop back at her apartment before we did so. From the closet of the entryway, she pulled out the thing that took up the most room. It was a grand picnic basket, complete with wineglasses and a space for the bottle of red we took along. We hauled the thing to Luxembourg Gardens, taking turns shouldering its weight.

The day was cool, a slight wind cutting through our clothing and playing with the ends of the scarf I'd borrowed. I hadn't expected to stay in Europe so late into the fall, so I was mostly living in a pair of lined pleather pants.

Elise and I sat down on a gingham blanket, the chill of the ground seeping up from below. It was only after we had our plates heaped with figs and fine sharp cheese, that a guard came to scold us. There were chairs scattered throughout the garden, Elise translated for me, but it was forbidden to sit on the grass. I looked at Elise, and we began to gather our things. The guard bounced the rifle on one shoulder while we did so, as if for emphasis.

"He was very, very serious about the condition of Marie de Médicis' lawn," Elise huffed, as we made our exit. Much later, we'd learn that there were designated areas for picnicking in the park and that the guard hadn't cared enough to mention them.

The next morning found us at Paris' bird market. It was only held on Sundays, when the famed Marché aux Fleurs closed for a day and was taken over by rows of cages. Elise and I walked between the metal enclosures, gawking at the captives' plumage.

"I've been thinking about getting a budgie or something," Elise admitted, "but where will I put it?"

It was the stuffed zebra at a dinner party all over again.

"Maybe in your next apartment," I suggested.

"Maybe," she agreed.

We walked at a steady pace, until a man selling birdseed stopped us both. He seemed normal enough at first, until we noticed the animal perched on his shoulder. It was not a bird, but an enormous white rat. The rat wore a tiny, red, plaid cap.

Alberta, where Elise and I were both from, introduced a rat control program in the 1950s after the rodents were discovered on a farm in the province. A control zone was put in place, stretching some six-hundred kilometres along the Saskatchewan border. It remains to this day, as does the law that decrees it illegal to keep rats as pets. So, to see a man snuggling up to one of them was particularly unusual for both of us.

"I've never even seen one in this city," Elise whispered to me.

I could abide being hissed at by geese as I tried to get into my car. I could live with having my flowerbeds regularly torn apart by deer—the zinnias all bent in the spot they'd decided to bed down for the night. Even the occasional moose loping through the southern neighbourhoods of my city was a normal sight on local news. But rats were completely foreign to me, and not in a romantic way.

Elise and I left the market and headed to the banks of the Seine. We stopped along the way for cheese and wine before setting ourselves up on a free bench along the river. The day was pleasant and windless, the damp chill that had begun to seep into my bones finally dissipating. We toasted to the weather with wine and noticed something amiss only then.

At first, it seemed as if the cobblestones were moving. But the grey forms were not rocks at all. They were rats. They looked to be coming from the water, as if they'd hatched beneath the surface of it and were now emerging full grown. The river cruise boats chugged past at a slow pace. They were close enough to shore that Elise and I could hear the gasps of the tourists on them. They were safe out in the water, but what about when they had to return to shore?

I brought my feet up beside me on the bench and peered between the slats in the seat as the rats flowed beneath in a tiny, furred sea. The woman on the bench nearest ours sipped calmly at a tallboy of beer between gales of delighted laughter. She pointed at my feet and exclaimed, "You're wearing exactly the right sort of footwear for this." I glanced down at the big black boots that laced halfway up my shins and had to agree.

Elise and I packed up in a hurry. We worried the creatures might climb up the bench and onto our laps. When there was a slight break in the roiling flow, we leapt to two patches of bare ground.

"I swear I've never seen a rat here before," Elise repeated.

"Well, you have now," I countered.

We ran, the squeaks following in our wake only slightly muffled beneath the clomping heels of my boots.

The date of my flight out of Paris loomed large ahead. In my inaction, I had made my choice. But there was something else too. I was ready to go home. I landed back in Edmonton, glad for a bit of familiarity after so many months away. The days passed idly as I thought back to all I'd seen and grew grateful even for the most manic of my memories..

Eight days after I left, the concert I'd waffled about attending went ahead. Eagles of Death Metal played to one thousand five-hundred people at the Bataclan Theatre—ninety of whom died. Concertgoers were trapped inside for hours. At the end of a police standoff, survivors had to step over the bodies of the dead to get out.

I learned of other attackers who'd fired on the city's crowded cafés and restaurants and lay awake until Elise messaged to say she was safe. Though in the back of my mind, I still wondered what had become of those singing men from Budapest.

That Business with Eve

My mother always has something to say about the trips I take, and my journey to Ukraine was no different.

"Perhaps you shouldn't go," she fretted.

"What's the worst that could happen?" I asked, giving her thin upper arm a reassuring little squeeze.

"The conflict spreads and you find yourself in the middle of it?"

"I'll keep an eye on the news."

I knew going to Ukraine was risky, but I was afraid if I didn't go now, I might never get to see the country my ancestors had emigrated from.

"I'll pray for you every day that you're gone," my mother promised.

And I knew, with no small amount of guilt, that she would.

As I packed on the night before I was to leave, my partner admitted he wasn't thrilled with my travel plans either.

"I want to tell you not to go," he confided, "but I know if I do, you'll just stay longer."

"I'll be careful."

"No," he said, as he pressed his forehead against mine, in that way I loved. "You won't."

I flew into Kyiv following a short stay in Budapest and had barely stepped off the plane before a young man, who would later introduce himself as Mikhail, approached me. He wore a grin beneath his straw fedora.

"You're not from around here, are you?" he asked.

"No, I'm from Canada."

"Ride with us," he offered, and gestured to the three people flanking him. "We'll make sure you get where you're going." Visions of all my mother's possible worst-case scenarios appeared in my mind. I had not even collected my luggage and already I was in trouble.

"I think I'm okay, but thanks," I replied, and began to back away, clocking the exits as I did so. One of the women at his side stepped forward gingerly, as if afraid to spook me.

"These are good people," she promised, in an accent that I would later learn was from Chicago. "They're a bit over-friendly perhaps, but they mean well."

Disarmed and unsure of how to navigate my way from the airport to Kyiv, I soon found myself in a Soviet-era van with defunct seatbelts, speeding down the highway in what I hoped was the direction of the apartment I had subletted. When we did arrive at the building, the instructions to get inside were written in Russian.

"How would you have gotten in without us?" Mikhail asked.

"Well, I had planned to buy a phone card before some crazy Russian accosted me at the airport."

After the apartment owner handed off the keys, my new friends followed me inside, and I wondered if they were planning on staying. They checked the sturdiness of the deadbolts before Mikhail finally declared, "It's much nicer than I thought an apartment in this area would be. You can stay here."

"Great," I deadpanned.

"We'll meet up with you tomorrow in the city," he informed me.

When they were gone, I nipped over to a bank to get some hryvnias. As I stood waiting for my cash, I remembered I had seen the currency before. On a train ride some years earlier, I'd ended up talking to a man from Montenegro who insisted I had to visit Ukraine, given my background. He'd passed me a little blue bill and said, "It's only enough for a coffee or something, but it'll get you started."

I hadn't known then this would be the overarching theme of my experience in the country: men telling me things I needed to do. And that, for reasons I can't explain now, I would sometimes listen to them.

The following day I got lost in Kyiv's subway system. The Cyrillic name for each station was printed in waist-high letters, while the Roman equivalent was displayed in a miniscule font often around corners. Many stations had two names, so I would spend thirty minutes below ground, circling hallways as well-meaning people gestured to the right and left with smiles, before realizing I'd been in the right spot all along.

On the trains, station names were called out both in Russian, as well as bastardized-Russian for those of us more likely to read it that way. I stood tittering, thinking of the girlfriend I'd visited in Paris and the game that she'd made up of reading every very French-sounding metro station in the most Anglo-Saxon way she could.

I discovered Arsenalna in Kyiv is the deepest metro station in the world. The escalators ran twice as fast as the ones I was used to, as if you were leaping into the earth. Regardless, it still took some time to get to the bottom. Some passengers sat down on the steps for the wait, their long, fashionable coats dangling so close to the speeding steps that I had to close my eyes. I called Mikhail to tell him I was lost and would catch up with him later in the week.

"Where are you?" he demanded. "We'll come find you."

"That's just the thing. I don't know."

With the help of a few passing strangers, I discovered I was still in Arsenalna. I had just taken a wrong turn and was in a different tunnel.

I went with Mikhail and his posse out of the city to a nearby village. On one of the trains we took, a young man in a tattered jacket playing the accordion pushed himself into the packed train car and began to serenade us.

"Only in Ukraine," yelled Mikhail, as the accordionist sidled up right behind us. Strangers pushed money at the racket-making man and shoved him back out onto the platform when the train stopped again.

Mikhail had grown up in Russia and been born when it was still part of the USSR. Though he'd moved to Seattle many years before, he kept coming back to Ukraine, and to the family he had here.

"What about Russia?" I asked him. "Do you go there much?"

"Only in the winter. That's the only time of year it's nice. There are too many bugs in the summer."

"It sounds like Alaska."

"Exactly."

We arrived at Mikhail's cousin's house where, much like an East Coast party, festivities were taking place in the kitchen. Chairs materialized from somewhere, and a stranger poured me a shot of vodka and told me to eat. I did so, but not to the host's liking.

"Eat more," Mikhail urged, filling a plate with tiny sandwiches for me. Across the table, his sister, a fetching blonde, baptised herself in a shot of pepper vodka before departing for bed.

After we'd gotten sufficiently drunk and eaten our body weight in salted fish, Mikhail and I went out into the cool night air to smoke beside a tank commander. Though I had abstained from cigarettes for the past year, I grew tired of being pestered and lit up too.

"It's probably not even real tobacco," Mikhail assured me.

"Sure. Anything that's mojito flavored can't possibly be bad for you."

As we smoked, the tank-driver regaled us with a story. He'd grown up in the village where we now stood and had lived across the street from a boy his own age until they both turned seventeen, when that boy moved away to Russia. Three years later, the tank-driver received a letter from his old friend.

"How can you stay in Ukraine?" the man had written. "They eat children there."

A few nights later, I followed Mikhail, his sister, and some of their young cousins to a medical-themed bar with a back-alley entrance. Inside, the bartenders were dressed as orderlies in blue scrubs. The waitresses flitted through the crowd in white nurse's uniforms, though the garments were sexless and vaguely communist—as if they'd been bought in bulk and all in the same size, and so they fit no one. The girl who served us shots of hard liquor in test tubes had a faded stain at the waist of her uniform that resembled old blood.

From where we sat, I caught a glimpse of a fireball erupting into the air.

"What's going on?"

"Calm down," Mikhail scolded, leading me to the bar.

A woman sat wearing a fire-retardant vest and a helmet that was on fire. Nearby, an unhurried bartender fixed her a shot. The woman drank it, then received several strikes on the head with a stick before the blaze was finally snuffed out.

"Do you want to do it?" Mikhail asked.

"I don't think anyone should drink a beverage that requires them to put on protective headgear first."

"Chicken."

After Mikhail's cousins showed me the best way to debone a fish in the nearly pitch-black bar, we left. The night was warm, and the streetlights cast a soothing sort of haze that blurred with my own drunkenness until everything seemed a misty yellow. The pop of colour that was the Red University beckoned to us in the monochromatic landscape. We all piled onto the benches outside the bright building, tipsily waiting for cabs that would ferry us home.

An elderly poet came up to us then. He was white-haired and walked with a noticeable limp. He glanced at me for only a fleeting second before turning to Mikhail's beautiful sister and lowering himself onto one knee before her. In this position of supplication, he began to recite his poetry.

"It's mostly in Polish," Mikhail said, "so I really don't know what he's saying. Still, pretty cool though, right?"

I agreed that it was.

When the poet finished, he had to be helped to his feet. We applauded and he bowed deeply before striding away, the hitch in his gait seeming a little less pronounced now. I felt certain he was on his way to romance someone else, and that he would continue in this pilgrimage until morning.

I caught up with Mikhail a few days later at a baptism for a member of his extended family. I'd tried to beg off, saying it sounded like a private matter, and I'd already included myself in too many of these, but he wouldn't hear of it.

"You have to see a baptism while you're here," Mikhail insisted.

"Why?"

"Because you're here to experience the culture," he pressed, though I couldn't remember saying anything of the sort to him.

Admittedly, I was curious about the ceremony. Back in Canada, I'd attended Orthodox funerals, but never a baptism. Those who kept the old beliefs were dying off without replacement.

There were about twenty of us gathered inside a small, high-ceilinged room in the village church. The building was constructed of dark wood, the planks in tight formation all the way to the high octagon-shaped ceiling.

As I stood in the sweltering space, I glanced at the other women around me, feeling underdressed. They wore headscarves, and so did I thanks to Mikhail's instruction, but mine was part of a makeshift costume loaned to me by yet another one of his cousins. One scarf was draped over my hair, and another was knotted around my waist to hide my black jeans.

Two men entered the room and poured water from a white plastic pail into a gilded basin at the front. The service hummed along in Ukrainian, and I caught only the bits that Mikhail translated to me in snatched whispers.

The baby cooed near us, fussing a little in his father's arms. It was only after the priest submerged the infant in the basin—the child's surprised wails filling the room—that the mother was allowed to join the congregation.

"Why wasn't she here before?" I asked Mikhail.

"The birth of a child is considered a sin in the Orthodox Church. This woman has not been allowed to attend service since giving birth to her son. Only after his baptism can she be re-introduced to the church, and I suppose forgiven."

"But why just the mother?"

"Oh, you know," he said waving me off. "Because of that business with Eve and the apple."

The mother positioned herself before the priest for her public absolution, with her infant son now silent in her arms. The baby busied himself by tugging her headscarf off again and again, exposing her shining hair to the brilliance of the sun yawning in the church's high windows.

After the ceremony finished, Mikhail and I stood off to one side, eavesdropping on a conversation between the father of the baptised child and the priest.

"You'll like this," Mikhail observed, "the father just offered to dump the water in the basin outside, but the priest refused him, saying its holy now. It will be used to water the church's plants."

We filed out and re-congregated in a covered outdoor area with long wooden tables. I didn't really know any of these people, and yet they filled my glass with vodka again and again as we toasted to the baby's future, to the mother's health, and to new friends. I was seated between Mikhail and a man who claimed to have once been part of the Lithuanian mafia. The man was missing a few fingers, and I deigned not to ask how he'd been forced to part with them. His second wife, a woman sixteen years his junior, sat nearby in a bright red dress.

After I'd lost count of the toasts, the Lithuanian man confided, "My wife is forty now, and not so young anymore." He smoothed back his still-thick, greying hair with the truncated fingers of his mangled hand before admitting he was thinking of moving on to a third wife. "Perhaps," he suggested, "you would like to be the one to claim this position. I can promise you it will come with a great deal of travel."

All of this was relayed to me through Mikhail, who'd been translating the conversation. Now, he turned to face me awkwardly on our shared bench seat. "I think you should consider his offer," he weighed in, "I mean, really, what else have you got going on?"

"You do realize I have someone waiting for me at home, right?"

"Oh sure, the guy who let you come to Ukraine alone."

"Nobody 'lets' me do anything," I countered, but already he'd returned to ignoring me.

The Lithuanian man's current wife brought him a cup of tea and when it arrived, he pointed to me and said, "Get her a cup as well." The wife gave me a dirty look and I trained my gaze on a spot somewhere over her left shoulder. The tea was delivered with a slice of cake, and the man insisted that we share it. I tried to decline but Mikhail shushed my protests.

As we dug our forks into the fluffy slice, the man grew even more animated. "My mother possessed a gift," he explained. "She had been able to divine whether one's first child would be male or female, and I inherited this ability."

He requested I give him my hand. I extended my open palm. The man briefly examined the lines on it before professing, "You will have a baby girl first." Then, he clasped my fingers in his and said, "And I would like to be the one to give her to you."

The next morning, I woke up alone with a hangover that presented itself as an intricate latticework of knots bulging behind my eyes. The apartment I'd rented had enormous windows, sparsely covered with a few left-behind slats from what had once been a set of venetian blinds. Through the gaps, the daylight thundered in. I groped around the apartment for something to cover my eyes, and eventually fell back to sleep with a pair of black thong underwear on my head.

After recovering enough to go out, I ventured to Kyiv's system of underground churches and mummified priests. The priests had been laid to rest in tiny coffins made of glass. I thought it sounded like something from a fairy tale, but when I peered into one of the coffins, I saw only the shriveled skin of an exposed wrist peeking out from beneath sacred garments.

A guide led me through the twists and turns of the underground labyrinth, detailing the priests who'd been buried there. "Are you a believer?" she asked.

The hope in her face shone like a lantern down there in the dark. I skirted the truth and said only that I'd been brought up by Christians. She let the matter drop as we approached a coffin containing only the upper half of a priest.

"This man spent three decades of his life buried up to his waist in earth to help fight his desires," my guide recounted proudly.

Throughout this trip, I found myself furtively slipping into churches. I had put that sort of religion behind me some years before, having decided I didn't like the way it dictated what I could and couldn't do with my body and my life. To see this long-dead man, buried to his waist in earth put all too fine a point on those feelings.

Coming up into daylight, I strode in the direction of some of Kyiv's most famous murals. Many new works had gone up in response to the Euromaidan protests. I'd round a corner and there would be two or three decorating the concrete façades of Soviet-era structures, mirroring each other in blasts of swirling colour.

I passed a mural of a Ukrainian gymnast who'd spoken out against the annexation of Crimea, her head precariously near the painted grass as she tumbled through air. Another showed a woman in a traditional shirt, a vyshyvanka, with trees bisecting her. I saw one I'd passed before, of a girl rendered in shades of blue wearing a flower crown. One of her giant hands rested atop a city, while the other cradled a boy who stared at her as if in awe.

Mikhail had offered to take me around to the murals, but I knew how easily I could be distracted in his presence. Instead, we'd arranged to meet up at the train station after I'd finished, though, by the time I did, I was turned around and nowhere near the trainline. A young man in tinted glasses tried to show me where to go with hand gestures, but when I looked at him cluelessly he decided to escort me instead.

"I'll figure it out," I tried to protest, but he assured me, via Google Translate, that he was headed in the same direction anyway.

It wasn't long before the man's phone piped up again to ask whether I had a boyfriend.

I told him I did.

He persisted via automated voice, asking, "Are you sure you really have a boyfriend?"

"Yes," I confirmed, and, seeing he wasn't going to let up, I told a white lie. "I'm meeting him at the train station."

"So, you're going to meet your mother?" he ventured, trying a tactic entirely new to me.

"No, my boyfriend."

He left me when we were a block or so away from our destination, though not before he said in careful English, "You are very beautiful. Your boyfriend is very lucky."

I recounted this to Mikhail when we found each other. "I leave you alone for five minutes and this is what happens..." he said shaking his head in disapproval.

He drove us to the outskirts of the city, where we were to view a well-preserved village. As we got further out, the cars darting around us like distracted fish, I felt suddenly how deeply I would miss the place.

I was to leave the following day.

"Just stay," Mikhail coaxed.

"I can't," I told him, which was true. I had the feeling if I didn't leave soon, I never would.

The next day, I took a train that coasted through the Ukrainian countryside, arriving in the city of Lviv in the early evening. The apartment I'd secured—in a centuries-old building—wasn't far from the city square, and the nearby streets teemed with people. I dropped off my things and headed out into the blur of faces, where I noticed everyone was paired off. Couples held hands. Laughing girls in bright coats clicked on high-heels across uneven cobblestones, their arms resting in the crooks of those belonging to their more steady-footed partners. I ducked out of the fray into a shop to purchase a few things to get me through the night and skittered back to my apartment feeling very much alone.

I emerged the following morning into the bright sunlight of an early fall day. Soon, wedding parties spilled out of the churches and into the streets, on this, a Wednesday. Women in towering shoes promenaded with their grooms as their white dresses collected dirt from the streets. Bridesmaids, all of them in rose pink, stumbled to keep up and lift the fabric out of the muck.

I saw a wedding every day in Lviv. I got into the habit of sipping coffee in the cafés lining the streets and watching processions of brides. Dropped flowers from their bouquets floated by in the breeze. Limos crawled past with screaming bridesmaids seated on the window ledges in the rear of the car, protesting the bumps in the road as they slid around in their silk dresses.

I felt lonely. I had already been missing my partner, but I'd had Mikhail and his family to distract me from that feeling. Now, lost in a sea of matrimonial bliss, I became aware of the ache.

On the third day of my visit, I waited outside a particularly ancient church while the couple inside said their "I dos." When the newlyweds emerged, I stood awkwardly off to one side. The bride tossed candy into the streets, her eyes catching mine as she tried to place me. I slipped in the door as the procession moved off, the smell of recently extinguished candles still thick in the air.

"Do you think you could maybe get on a plane?" I asked my partner later that night on the phone.

"I can't just up and leave."

"I know. It is lonely here without you though."

"Of course it is," he said. "I'm amazing."

The next day, I floated through the city square and spotted several mannequins in wedding gowns. One was attached to a door by a thick length of chain, leaning slightly as if straining against her bonds. Another hung from a balcony, as if the pressure of her upcoming nuptials had proved too much for her. A third stood, handless and slightly filthy from the wind, next to a red Lada. Her expression, rendered in plastic, was one of certainty. If she just waited there long enough, dressed in her finery, surely someone would take her away from all of this.

I admired the plunging neckline of one particularly ornate little number and noticed a twenty percent off sign on it. The dress glittered with hundreds of tiny seed pearls, and I barely resisted the urge to test the weight of it, knowing it would never fit in my backpack.

I decided all of this was only the frequency illusion in action: after noticing something once, you're more likely to spot it again and again. It was pure coincidence that, at every café, the tables surrounding mine were full of couples handfeeding each other with fingers that moments later disappeared under the cloths covering their tables.

Remembering the kind urgings of a woman I'd met on the train from Kyiv, I tried to shake off the blues I was feeling by booking a ticket to that evening's ballet.

"Did you mean two tickets?" the woman at the desk asked.

"No," I said firmly. "Just one."

At the Lviv National Opera, I found myself seated next to two well-dressed men. They stood politely and smiled as I took the only other chair in our row. Then, as the lights dimmed for the show, I watched, afire with jealousy, as they clasped each other's hands and snuggled closer together.

The following day, I visited Lviv's High Castle Park. From the top of the hill, I could see the city in its entirety. It was windy that high up, and I felt nervous and untethered, my scarf nearly whipping free before I tucked it in. I gazed out at the roofs of buildings I didn't recognize and felt the beauty of the place like a tangible thing in my chest.

As if out of the ether, a couple materialized at my shoulder and began to kiss. I ignored them at first, until they became more passionate, and began to swoon in my direction. The girl's long hair slapped against my face in the wind as I took my leave. They were too lost in each other and the setting to notice anyone else.

That night on the phone, our voices crackling with distance, my partner asked, "Are you sure you'll be ready to come home in a week?"

"Yes. I'm absolutely certain."

I hung up and leaned back in my chair on the balcony, watching as a thin black cat performed its highwire act from apartment to apartment via the gutters. Sometimes, it came close and allowed me to scratch its head. Its company was some consolation in a city like Lviv, where everyone seemed to come in pairs, but it was time to go. Time to go and be with those I loved most.

"Just make the dirt look even."

Let's Draw Straws

At eighteen, I got a job working as a waitress at a steakhouse in my hometown. I was an awkward girl and tried to hide beneath a thick coating of makeup and a matted red beehive the way a full-grown bear might duck behind the thin stalks of a dead tree. I hadn't yet gotten used to myself and had no understanding of what it meant to have breasts, as they had only just arrived. Like a relative who brings far too much luggage, I felt I just didn't have the room for them. I didn't know you could get something caught in the place between the fleshy underside of your chest and your rib cage, and spend the day with it there, oblivious. In the dimly lit staff bathroom, I'd peer into the mirror, agog, as I lifted and scraped at dried sour cream with moistened paper towel that came apart in my fingers.

This action reminded me of the elderly women whom I swam laps with at the town pool. They would shower nude as I quickly rinsed myself off, still in my bathing suit, and tried not to look as they lifted and washed under each sagging mammary with the sort of vicious circular strokes one uses to clean bugs off a windshield. There was one who, after her shower, would tuck a towel under her arms but leave it hanging open. Then she would stand in the middle of the vanity counter blow-drying her pubic hair and talking to me about the weather, her grandchildren, things her doctor said, while I tried to quickly gather my makeup, the mascara tube seeming to jump from my hand and skitter across the floor.

My feelings of inadequacy at work were amplified by the clientele. I served mostly roughnecks, men who wandered in wearing mud-stained overalls, with one strap unlatched to reveal a T-shirt depicting the silhouette of a pole dancer and the words "I support single mothers" underneath the graphic.

I was only a couple of weeks into the job when one of the rig guys pulled out his testicles to show them to another one of the waitresses. I looked over to see him waving what appeared to be a shaved gerbil at her. I'd never seen testicles before, particularly on such a viewing platform, his lifeline peeking out between the lose folds of skin. The girl got angry, while I had done what I knew best then, and fled for the relative safety of the kitchen.

The genital display prepared me for a later job where one patron liked to come in and eat dinner with his penis sitting outside the zipper of his jeans. It stayed there, as flaccid and strange as a pet squirrel in his lap until a former bouncer from the strip club across the street finally threw him out.

But even as I grew more used to the job and its customers, their interest always came as a surprise. A man I was serving would say something like, "You really remind me of my daughter," before sliding a twenty and his hotel room key across the table at me and reaching out to rest a hand on the small rise of one of my still-developing hips. I'd heard about other girls who'd take the key cards and ransack hotel rooms during the day when the men were at work. The cost of the missing TV, empty minibar and whatever else was worth stealing charged to the company card. But I didn't have the balls for such things. It took everything I had to shyly pull away from their open palms.

In moments like these, I was grateful for the company of my coworkers. Women who would take over the offending table in a heartbeat and seemed to know so much more about everything. One revealed the secrets of probiotic yogurt to me and, later, another urged me to wrap a few garlic cloves in cheesecloth and shove it into my vagina to cure the constant yeast infections we all got from our mandatory nude-coloured pantyhose. It would be years before I discovered the practical uses of thigh-high stockings.

In the middle of summer, during a heat wave, Faith advised me (in the middle of the dining room) to cut the crotch out of my nylons. The female customer directly to our right paused suddenly, her soupspoon halfway from the bowl to her mouth. Another waitress shushed us, but

I couldn't stop laughing. I did try Faith's suggestion, but it felt odd to have my pantyhose hanging from the clothesline, the gaping hole in the gusset billowing in the late summer wind as the neighbours sat in their backyard trying not to stare.

The job often left me with a raw feeling. One afternoon, the other girls and I stood around gossiping about an accident that had happened just outside of town. A man had gotten his arm caught in some sort of machinery and it had been torn right off, along with a couple of fingers from the opposite hand. "The paramedics were throwing up in the ditch it was so bad," Faith said over the rim of her coffee cup, her dark lipstick blurring into the lines around her mouth. Within a few years her husband would die in a work-related accident.

A week or so after that conversation, one of my favourite regulars came in. His left arm had been severed at the shoulder and, when he waved to me, I noticed a few fingers off his right hand were missing. Before the accident, he and his wife had used the restaurant as a place to fight. They'd come in and order cocktails and appetizers and look to everyone in the room like two people very much in love. Then, their voices would raise as some old scab was picked open. Suddenly, the wife would be out the front door, the glass doors of the vestibule slamming after her in the night wind. He would chase her, throwing a handful of bills in his wake to cover the tab and the trouble. If the performance had been dramatic enough, the other patrons in the dining room would clap.

Now, the man with the severed arm sat in subdued silence next to his wife, the ice in their waterglasses melting. I flitted about them until I couldn't take the tension anymore. "Something's different about you," I said. "You got a haircut, didn't you?"

And I've never been so glad as I was when great bubbles of tension-dissipating laughter erupted from them both.

For all the job's trials, the boss was probably the worst of them. He was always just a little too close, brushing the top of my ass with the open palm of his hand as he walked by. Though others had it worse than me. When one of the girls returned from her honeymoon, her skin a luminous sun-kissed brown, he asked to see her tan lines.

I convinced myself the boss meant nothing by his grazing fingers, that he had touched me again and again by mistake. When he did finally grab a handful of my ass and press me so hard into the corner of a deepfreeze that I had a triangle-shaped bruise on my pubic bone for weeks, I was actually surprised. I can still remember trying to balance on my tiptoes away from the meat of that hand, and the sound of Trudy, one of the cooks, laughing somewhere around the corner the way she did when she'd lost her teeth in someone's food.

Behind the frosted glass panels and low light of what had been the smoking side of the restaurant up until a couple of months before (my hometown being one of the last Canadian holdouts to resist the law), I told my boss to keep his hands to himself.

"This is just how I am with my girls," he explained, "how I've always been." His tone suggested I was passing up a rare opportunity.

"Well," I replied, my voice quaking with what I'd initially thought was fear, but soon recognized as the first snaking tendrils of rage, "it's not how you are with me."

As I'd known they would, my shifts became worse after that "talk." I worked more splits, more of the dead times when tips were sparser. But it didn't matter, I was on my way out. On one of the last summer days that I worked there, a strong wind kicked-up just before the lunch rush. I and the other waitresses scrambled to retrieve the huge green-and-white-striped umbrellas that dotted our patio. Inside, we counted them but came up one short. I went out again and found the boss staring at the roof of the gas station across the street. The missing umbrella jutted from it, festive as a drink garnish. I bent at the waist, screaming with laughter, and felt the heat of my boss's anger as he shoved past me.

I quit and got a job in a nearby city working for a woman named Opal. She was in her sixties and when she first hired me, seemed kindly. But I soon realized how quick she was to send people home when their skirts weren't short enough, or they weren't wearing enough makeup. The restaurant didn't have a dress code, but rather a list of strict clothing guidelines. Pants were not allowed but shorts were, as long as they didn't come past mid-thigh. Skirts and dresses followed this same rule. I watched long fake nails reach up under hemlines to scratch and thought of the health code violations. Every meal a Russian roulette-like chance to get gonorrhoea from a salad.

The other servers were unperturbed by their work wear, not caring if an ass cheek descended below the hem of their dresses when they leaned over to wipe the tables. They could take the abuse from men and comfortably wear their skimpy work outfits in a way I hadn't yet learned to and probably wouldn't. I found them rough and frightening.

Lola often complained about the wealthy male patron who would pay a thousand dollars for each breast shown to him in the relative privacy of the downstairs washroom. He had propositioned two of the waitresses on separate occasions and both had complied, rolling down one side of their tube tops and then the other before watching him write out a cheque. Lola's single mastectomy a few years earlier had cut her earning possibilities quite literally in half. I often thought about splitting the proceeds with her if he ever came my way, but there seemed to be something infinitely depressing about standing topless before a middle-aged man, listening to the toilet in the next stall just run and run.

But I soon realized I was unlikely to be one of the chosen anyway. At my first job my chest had been too large for my liking, but for this new place it was too small. One regular told me straight out that I had small tits. "Thanks," I fired back, "I got them from my father." Still, the comm ent stung, especially because Opal had begun to start off my shifts by suggesting I get breast implants. I heard this snippet of advice in my sleep for months after she had one of the other waitresses call and fire me.

After that, I was unemployed for a while, which lent me ample time to learn about different types of implants and what could go wrong. I found photos of implants that had hardened, leaving the owner with two perfectly round rocks protruding from her ribs. Another showed a set of fake breasts that had slowly moved away from each other, like displeased lovers, turning away. Though the deciding factor for me was the story of a woman whose left implant had suddenly burst. The saline had flooded through her body and left her with a vacant skin sack that resembled an empty sock. I imagined standing over a table with a pair of purchased breasts, reaching forward only to have one rupture. The sudden tide of water would stream over my rib cage, down my abdomen and finally form a puddle in my shoes.

After a long while, I got work through a friend at a crumbling Irish pub. I was unsurprised to find my new uniform included a pleated scrap of plaid that hardly covered my ass, a deep V-neck top made of an oily polyester that held scents like no fabric I'd ever known, a pair of knee-high socks, and black flats. I had the sense that as I aged, my uniforms would continue to shrink. I pictured myself in my eighties wearing a couple of Band-Aids and a well-placed scarf.

The pub resided in an area of the city where skinny, barren lots went for a million dollars. Out front, there was a juncture referred to as Poo Corner by the locals. A drunken city planner had explained the smell to me once. The city's sewage funnelled down to that very corner and pooled there, wafting its fetid scent over some of the city's most coveted real estate. It was, he claimed, the smell of affluence.

Inside, the bar always reeked of sewage. Customers complained about it endlessly and yet kept coming back, as if they couldn't help themselves. It reminded me of something I'd read once: that the best perfumes always have a little bit of shit in them. Some customers seemed not to notice the pernicious funk and had sex in the toilets anyway, the half-inch of yellowish water on the floor soaking into their shoes and doing little to deter their boozy ardour. Plumbers were brought in, men who told us we'd have to level the place and start all over again to deal with the problem. Instead, we limped on, burning air fresheners at a steady clip and enduring the constant respiratory infections we all kept getting.

Inside the bar itself, fruit flies swarmed the beer taps. Patrons flapped their hands to clear the hovering clouds over their beverages. In shallow pools of beer, mice swam languidly across the floor. Too drunk to run, they were easily swept up into dustpans. In the kitchen, a flying ant infestation had taken up residence in the coffeemaker. I'd gone to put in fresh grounds one morning, and they'd come spilling out, several flying right into my open mouth.

A pipe burst, forming a sinkhole beneath the bar's dishwasher. The spongy tile went undetected until one of the stockier employees sank through the floor to his knees. The owner was forced to re-tar the foundation as the customers sipped on, paying no mind to this new, slightly more toxic smell.

When a customer of mine knocked over a flaming shot of Chartreuse and lit his table on fire during construction, I stood watching the flames lick at the booze for a long time—their orange tongues perilously close to the dirt-crusted bric-a-brac that lined the walls—before finally tossing him a wet rag to put it out.

When one of the weekend bouncers insisted he'd found a deer leg in the toilet in the men's washroom, I didn't believe him. He detailed the tableau: the limb hoof-up, with the thigh jammed into the hole at the base, the bowl oddly devoid of blood.

"Get outta here," I said, swatting him lazily with a billfold.

Yet, when I arrived the next morning, there was the leg, jammed through the slats of the pallet out back like a furry warning. I refused to carry it to the dumpster. By the end of the day, it had migrated again to beneath the door handle of the bar manager's car, bent at the knee at an oddly sexual angle.

I often didn't mind the job, but when I wiped down tables in a skirt so short it prevented me from bending over for fear it would expose the entirety of my ass, I couldn't help but feel ridiculous. On the occasions when the bar ran out of things, I'd sometimes find myself in line at the grocery store, holding a fist full of limes and tugging at the hem of my mini while people around me pretended not to stare. "Yes," I often wanted to say to no one in particular, "this is what an adult looks like."

Most men at least took pity on me in my get-up, but some women punished me just for wearing it, especially the divorced ones who travelled in packs and appeared to dislike me for the sheer fact that their previous husband had run off with—or was about to run off with—a waitress. Some of these women enacted misplaced revenge by sending me back to the kitchen with their food orders over and over again, their medium-rare steaks blackening to a well-done strip of meat that curled on the plate like a sneer. They would arrive in overly-perfumed groups, wafting past as I stood with the other waitress on shift, drawing straws for who would have to serve their party. The women usually drank Chardonnay, and their glasses were forever raised in the air, signalling for my attention as if calling over a dog that has shit in a particularly expensive pair of shoes. And as I short-poured their wine from behind the bar, I wondered what had happened to the idea of female solidarity.

Much of the bar's clientele was elderly, and a few had not missed a happy hour in thirty years. Sometimes, they just disappeared one afternoon and never returned, having sipped their last pint. Stuffed animals that had once belonged to deceased patrons lined the back bar, permanently welded in place with spilled liqueur.

I still remember Fergal, a foul-tempered senior who would verbally abuse me and try to order things that weren't on the menu until he'd had his three-beer limit. After that, he would try to take me home with him to his assisted-living facility up the block. "You know, I haven't had a woman since my wife died," he'd say, as he pushed a single loonie my way, the sound of it scraping loudly across the bar top.

"I can't imagine why. Do you want me to call you a cab?" I'd ask.

"It's the feminine touch that I miss," he'd continue wistfully, not having heard me.

"And I miss believing that college was my ticket out of here."

One afternoon Fergal fell off his stool. He returned an hour later to retrieve the shoe that had fallen off when he'd gone down. It was winter and around -30°C outside, and I'd wondered how he'd made it all the way home in the bitter cold without noticing one of his feet was bare. Soon afterward, he stopped coming in.

Fergal's title of oldest patron was passed to Morris, an elderly ukulele player who never got out of his pajamas and performed inuendo-filled songs about the days when he'd seen flowers everywhere. Morris had once fallen in the bath one long weekend, breaking his hip. Come Tuesday, his homecare worker had found him still in the water, pneumonic and half-alive, his submerged skin ruched into mountainous ridges. Morris had come out of that tub groping, and I might have felt threatened had he been able to do anything more than swat me ever so gently on the bum. His slender blue-white hands had all the force of a butterfly landing on my rump.

Towards the end of his tenure at the pub, Morris began to urinate on chairs, leaving shallow pools in his wake.

Anywhere else, it would have been a pungent sort of graffiti, but here we hardly noticed unless someone else sat in it. One night, he wet himself on a cushioned stool. At the suggestion of one of the bartenders—who'd refused to help—I tried to hose it off in the dish pit, and quickly realized my folly. I set the chair next to the dumpster out back, but when I came in to open the following morning it was gone. A few days after that, it turned up by the dumpster again, the salvagers having figured out that the furniture of purgatory belongs nowhere else.

Morris died a couple months later. In his absence, I found myself wondering if the guy who did our Open Mic Night (a man who played so loud I later blamed him for my tinnitus) experienced a lot of overlap between the bar and his day job as a mortician. I found out about his other gig one night when he'd grumbled to me about one of the musicians tacking gum to his music stand. "This is really disgusting," he said, as I handed him a butter knife, "and I wired a guy's face back together this morning."

All the staff were expendable. We knew we could be terminated for gaining weight or deciding to continue a pregnancy. When one of the girls broke her front teeth falling in front of the bar, we worried the owner would come in and sack her before she could afford to have them capped. Our bodies were groped and spoken about as if they were city property. For a while, there was even a customer who'd throw me over one shoulder, exposing my ass to the room beneath the job's regulation miniskirt. He'd carry me out of the bar while drumming a song unknown to me on the back of my thigh. Disappointment bloomed in my chest every time he turned around and headed back.

Every week or so, I'd get an offer from one of the customers: two hundred dollars for a hug, a new laptop for some photos of myself, or fifty bucks for my socks. The socks, I sold.

Once, a portly redhead picked up one of my hands and asked me, "Do men often obsess about the distance between your joints?" It hadn't seemed pertinent at the time to tell him that they only did when they drove hatchbacks, as he did, and wanted to know if I'd fit into their trunks. When I pulled away, he'd been incredulous. "I'm not the sort of man who needs to masturbate in public," he railed, as if this explained everything. The next time he came in, he had a measuring tape with him. I wouldn't let him hold it against me, but he kept dropping it off the edge of the table to get a better idea of the length of my legs.

Then there was the immensely tall man who'd followed me home. He'd walked a few steps behind me and insisted he wasn't tailing me, but rather that his mother lived in this direction too. A few days later, he left a box full of chocolate-covered homemade cherry bombs on my doorstep. As I lit them and threw them off a nearby bridge, listening to the sound of their ricocheting blasts, I wondered if they were a gift or a threat.

Perhaps it was my total lack of professionalism that had invited the overture. One of the male regulars, a nurse, would lift the hem of my skirt beneath the shadow of the bar top and give me my shots for a vitamin deficiency after last call, the preservative stinging the meat of my thigh. The sensation was particularly pronounced if the nurse had had one too many. The tall man with the bombs learned of these events somehow, and on Halloween, he chased me to my car while wearing a Jolly Green Giant costume. "I've learned how to give injections," he yelled after me, "and I'm ready and waiting if you ever need me to."

"It could be worse," Max, one of the female bartenders said to me after I told her about the exchange. "I came home once to find a present from some patron on my pillow at my parents' house. They said they hadn't even seen anyone come in."

As she talked, I thought about one customer I'd mistakenly told of a recent break-up. When I showed up to work a few days later, there was a box waiting for me, wrapped in a black plastic garbage bag. Inside was a vibrator in bright Kelly Green.

Max insisted there were other ways to take revenge on the power imbalance that existed between us and the customers. When she'd worked at a concert venue, she was notorious for kicking out people's legs when they wouldn't move for her. She'd worn big black combat boots for the job, their meaty soles leaving mottled indigo reminders behind. "The first kick is a warning," Max advised sagely. "If that doesn't do it, I get 'em behind the knees. Makes them fold up like a cheap lawn chair."

On a night she and I were working together, she'd watched a woman pull on the greasy end of my braid to get my attention. I turned around, my mouth hanging open at her gall. The offending patron didn't notice the look on my face. She ordered another drink and the bill.

"Throw her out, or I'll do it," Max admonished me.

"She's leaving anyway," I said. "Best to just let her go."

"If you just put up with this shit it'll make you crazy, you know that, don't you?"

She was right of course. Not long after that incident, I slapped an Irishman for commenting on how slutty waitresses are. When I didn't get fired, I knew I wouldn't stop. Weeks later, when another man—someone who'd once flipped up my skirt under the guise of checking if there was anything underneath—began to yell that he'd heard I was easy, I slipped off my shoe and, while balancing on one leg, beat him about the back of the head with it.

"Why are you doing this?" he asked, as he cowered beneath another blow.

"Because if I'd just thrown the shoe at you," I explained, as I wound up for another strike, "you'd have built it into a goddamn shrine."

Soon after that, when a man was rude to me, I returned to him with two pints of beer and held them up to the light. "Now," I said, peering into their depths, "which of these do you suppose I peed in?"

I'd misjudged my mark though. After the offending man sipped his beer, he looked at me and said, "Miss, there's either too much urine in this beer or," and here he paused for effect, "not enough."

One night, a group of guys came into the bar and started a fight with some of the regular patrons. From behind the waist-high protection of the bar's wooden counter, I watched torn clothing land in a bloody pool on the floor in front of me. The sound of men hitting each other echoed the wet slapping noise of raw meat tossed onto the grill.

Eventually, the interlopers retreated, and the bartender and I barred the doors behind them. Through the pub's tiny front windows, we watched the strangers tear apart the deck of the house next door, a place that belonged to some retired nuns. The men began to circle the bar with 2x4s slung over their shoulders. I called the police. As we waited for them to arrive, the patrons grew restless. "You can't keep us here forever," one of them insisted, as we heard one of the men outside tug on the door.

"Dude," I said, exasperated, "it's for your own good."

When the squad car finally showed up three-quarters of an hour later, it did so with its sirens blaring from blocks away. The men got away, and I found myself filing a police report that gave me little faith. Weeks later, when the police called back looking for Bubbles (having taken my fake nametag as gospel), I told them she'd left town.

The clientele continued to get weirder. During the holiday season, a guy tried to organize a raffle of servers' panties to raise money for a Christmas children's charity that collected toys for kids. He claimed to be an auctioneer of some sort. After he suggested the raffle, he thought it logical for all of us to sleep with him—I guess because we already wouldn't be wearing underwear—and we had to throw him out.

"Sounds charming," Max said, when I told her about it later.

"He kind of was. At least he was trying."

"You draw in the weirdos though," she told me, as if it were somehow my fault that, several months before, a man had tried to convince me he'd been the one to discover the single remaining Avro Arrow frozen into the ice of Greenland.

"If I didn't chat these people up, I wouldn't know about a certain sect of people who think there are twelve Jesuses and three of them are holograms. Or about the meth addict who thought the government was sneaking into her house while she slept and sewing diseases into her clothes."

"Wasn't that also the girl that got bear-sprayed in the face and spent the rest of that night breaking into people's yards to use their garden hoses?" Max asked.

"One and the same."

It was true I was guilty of getting too involved. I'd once had a regular suffer a small heart attack right in front of me while I was polishing glasses at the bar. The man next to him got his heart pumping again with chest compressions while I was on the phone with paramedics. The momentarily dead regular straightened his vest and said, by way of explanation, "Sometimes when I drink alcohol, my heart stops because of the medication I'm on."

He operated a sort of halfway house for the bar staff. The most memorable of these housemates was a girl who paid her rent by making Jiffy Pop topless. After we closed on the hottest summer nights, I too had treated his nearby pool as if it were my own and dove in while wearing all my clothes.

When the colour returned to his face, he ordered another beer, and, against my better judgment, I gave it to him. An hour later, when I realized he was no longer in the pub, I found myself running to his unlocked house down the street, combing through stale-smelling rooms, wondering exactly where my responsibilities as his server ended. On my way back to the bar, I stopped to describe the patron I was looking for to a man who was unloading his car. "Did he walk out on his tab?" the man asked.

"Well, yes, but I'm more worried that he might be dead," I said, more flippantly than I felt.

The regular turned up the next day, as if nothing had happened, and things chugged along that way for some time, until he drove into the side of one of the other servers' cars and refused to hand over his insurance. The police were called, and we issued the thing that we bandied about more than any other bar: a lifetime ban.

Someone hired, for a time, an alcoholic chef, a man who quickly took to drinking the kitchen wine, a substance both not meant for drinking and stored at a temperature just below boiling. The chef had gotten one too many modified orders one night and threw knives at Max and me when we tried to enter the kitchen. Each time the saloon-style door swung open; he fired several more blades into the air with poor accuracy. He would not be placated, so we closed the kitchen and waited for him to leave.

As time marched on, I felt an almost motherly instinct for my coworkers brewing inside, particularly for the young ones who reminded me so much of myself. I saw them, standing in the middle of the room unsure of what to do next, their thin arms akimbo, their legs bent in a stance so awkward and familiar it almost hurt to look at it. This patron or that one reaching for them, and their visible unsureness of how to remove the hand from their bodies without causing a fuss. It made me feel so old when I wandered up to ask, "Is there a problem here?" while the newly surfaced varicose veins in my legs twitched.

I was starting to think it was time to get out, that I owed it to myself to leave before I forgot how. I was in this cycle of thought one afternoon while out watering the flowers that bordered the pub. I was just finishing up when a patron I knew well came rolling past on a children's tricycle. The man pulled up alongside me and skidded to a sloppy stop that suggested he had yet to make it home from the previous night's adventures.

"Get on my tricycle," he ordered me.

"I'm halfway through a shift," I told him, while visions of us toppling over onto my knees ran through my head.

"Come on," he slurred, wiggling an eyebrow, "I'll take you wherever you want to go."

I declined and left him there, half-toppled into the gutter, as I blinked my pupils wide again inside the dark bar. But as I stood polishing the hazy wineglasses I couldn't help wondering if it wasn't an escape I should've made. The two of us wobbling off into the late morning sun, the bar, and my life as I knew it getting further and further away, shrinking into the distance until it became something I could no longer see.

Brewed with Rage

While rounding the corner to thirty and still waitressing, I began to understand neither my body nor my patience would hold out much longer. The teens and early-twenty-somethings flitting past me seemed as bemused by my presence as I was—as if they'd come to work and found their mothers there.

After leaving a long-term bar job, I found myself at loose ends. In one interview, a manager scoffed when I told him I'd left my last position for my own safety. At another, the boss simply looked me up and down and told me he didn't have a job for me. In the third, I met Rodger, a man who favored crushed-velvet suits.

"It's your look I like," Rodger confided. "That's why I want to hire you."

I was too taken aback to respond. A decade before, my green hair and facial piercings had been a problem. Now they were a selling feature. The other manager, Todd, was less taken with me. "You're very pretty," he said, "but I don't know if you have enough personality to work here."

I sat across from him with my mouth slightly open. I was unsure of how to tell him that I had enough "personality" to understand he'd just called me stupid. In the end, he offered me the job anyway, though I was no longer sure I wanted it. I was told to wear black clothing and high heels.

"Heels," I repeated dumbly.

"Yeah, but only, like, two-inch ones," Rodger cooed brightly. His voice made it sound like he was presenting me with the gift of being slightly taller than my five-foot nine-inch height, and I'd just never considered the possibility before.

"I won't do it," I told them, thinking of the bunions that had already begun to deform my feet.

"Fine, but no sneakers," Todd acquiesced, as the faint smile on his face flickered and died.

When I arrived for my first shift, Rodger steered me out to the parking lot in a blood-coloured suit. "What do you see, Danica?" he asked.

"Cars?" I ventured, while trying to keep my teeth from chattering as the sharp wind blew gusts of cold air up my dress.

"Luxury cars," he corrected, pointing at the sleek metal shells. "Mercedes, Porsche, Ferrari. Our customers are of some status, and they expect to be served accordingly."

"Right," I agreed.

"You know, I drove by your place the other day."

"Why would you drive by my house?" I balked, peering into his rheumy, red eyes.

"I meant your old bar," he explained, his expression twisting into the very same one Todd had during our first meeting. "It's a cute little place."

"Sure, it is," I deadpanned, wanting him to know I understood he was lying.

Once back inside, I was paired with a short blonde who would show me the ropes. The first thing she asked was, "Are you cold?"

"A bit. It's chilly out there."

"Sure, but you're not going to keep that sweater on all night, are you?" she asked, her brows jumping to hide under perfect blunt-cut bangs.

"I was planning on it. Why?"

I turned as she swept the room with her arm, showcasing my new coworkers. I could see the pattern of everyone's bras through their shirts, and even from my place across the room, it was easy to make out the dark spheres of one girl's nipples.

"Oh," I said dumbly.

"Yeah."

The restaurant was a favourite lunch haunt for the wives of rich hockey players. These packs of bored women could put back bottle after bottle of wine, seemingly with little effect. When I offered to call them cabs, they laughed in my face, climbed into their Porsches, and sped off. DUIs were for poor people. People like me.

"Do you ever cut anyone off?" I asked one of the other servers.

"Nah, but once I had a dude fall asleep in a booth. I just covered him with a tablecloth and let him sleep it off."

"You do know that we're liable if we overserve patrons and they get into an accident, right?" I asked and felt suddenly very old.

She picked at a split end, half-listening.

"Yeah but, like, what are the odds of that?"

A few nights later, I closed the restaurant with a bartender who had the sort of sunburn that makes one think of calling an ambulance. All the while, she regaled me with the story of the ghost that haunted the building.

"I double and triple-check everything because of him," she explained, inspecting the dials on the kitchen range.

"How do you know it's a 'him'?"

"You don't watch the news?" she asked.

"Why does everyone think I'm stupid?" I hedged defensively.

She ignored me.

"A guy left here drunk one day and drove up onto the patio and into a table of people. He killed a kid."

"Jesus."

"Yeah, the driver said he'd been having a fight with his wife and was just distracted, but you and I know better. That's why the building has those pillars out front. New management put them in to keep it from happening again."

At home, I searched online for information on the incident. The driver had received only a four-month sentence for killing a two-year-old child. But, several months afterwards, some concerned local citizens decided that wasn't long enough. After kidnapping him, they cut off one of his thumbs with pruning shears.

When I came in for my next shift, a get-well card for Rodger was making the rounds. I signed in my usual incomprehensible scrawl and went to find Todd. "What happened to Rodger?" I asked when I found him perched beside a table of regulars.

"He had a hole in his intestines. Shit was pouring into his insides," Todd explained, before breaking into a long string of braying guffaws.

The regulars followed suit with nervous titters like boys in a locker room waiting for the next towel snap. As I strode away from their little gathering, I distinctly heard someone say the word *excrement* before peals of laughter erupted again.

Distressed, I cornered a co-worker in the kitchen.

"Should Todd really be sharing such private things about Rodger with everyone?" I asked her. "I wouldn't want the world to know if I was literally full of shit."

"Let me tell you a story," she replied, flinging the rolled cutlery in her hand into the bin in front of her. "A little while ago, one of the waitresses had a miscarriage in the staff bathroom. She hadn't even known she was pregnant, and the whole experience was very traumatic for her. After she left to go to the hospital, Rodger told everyone what had happened. The staff, the customers, everyone. So, I would guess that the consensus here, is that Rodger can go fuck himself."

"I didn't know," I bumbled to the back of her head, for she had already turned on the heel of her flat and was marching away from me.

As weeks passed, I noticed something about much of the restaurant's female clientele: they'd all had so much Botox that it was hard to discern their actual feelings about anything. I'd find myself staring at the motionless shelf of their eyebrows as we set about playing a game of "What's in This Drink That I Don't Like, and Could You Make It Without?"

A kind friend explained that, while I had been working in a bar dark enough to obscure every flaw, the world had become obsessed with injectables. "Even I get Botox every few months," she confided.

"Really?"

"Yep. I've been trying to get rid of my elevens."

"Elevens?" I repeated, imagining the human face as a paint-by-numbers canvas.

She pointed to the area between her eyebrows where there was the tiniest pair of twin indentations.

"These are called elevens," she clarified.

"If you say so."

One night I served a young woman whose lips squirmed on her face like fat worms slicked with lip gloss. She ordered perogies and I hovered to see how she would handle eating them with her over-injected lips.

"That will be all," the woman said primly, waving her fork to dismiss me.

I set about cleaning nearby, trying to watch out the corner of one eye as she speared a morsel and it disappeared into the puffed-up hole in her face.

"The kitchen wants you," one of the bartenders said, interrupting my gawking.

In the back, the cook with the word *skinhead* tattooed on his bald scalp asked, "How's your last table? Are they ready for me to start on their mains?"

"I suppose you might as well, but they are still working on the appetizer."

"It's been forty minutes."

"The lady at the table has cumbersome lip injections," I explained, my hand flitting in front of my mouth. "You should go out and take a peek."

"I'm good," he replied before returning to the stove. "I mean, why would you do that to yourself?"

Though I believed some of the clientele had taken things too far, I couldn't help but start to feel inadequate at work. I left home without my usual cardigans and began to hang out with everyone else in the back near the ovens. I layered my makeup more thickly, painting carefully around the metal ring in my lip while doing my best to ignore the chips it had taken out of my front teeth.

A couple of months into this, my partner cornered me.

"You're miserable," he said, inches from my mirrored face. "Why don't you quit, or at least look for something else?"

I was careful to finish extending my winged eyeliner into my hairline before I shook my head. "It's not that bad."

"Bullshit," he declared. "How about I come down for a beer? Then I'll get to see how you're really holding up."

I didn't want him to see how panicked I was on shift.

"No," I replied, "not tonight."

"Do you actually work there," he mused, "or are you seeing someone else?"

I knew he was kidding, but as I hoisted myself into a particularly tight skirt, we both understood the job was doing something to me.

That night, one of the two men I was chatting with asked, "What are you doing after work?"

"Oh, the usual," I answered flippantly. "I'm going to drive home and see if my boyfriend has moved all of my stuff out onto the front lawn in protest."

Both men went very quiet.

"What?" I asked.

One of them took a deep breath and explained, "My friend here recently got back from a trip to China and found all his things out on the grass. Twelve years of marriage and two kids and this is how his wife tells him it's over. It rained while he was away too. A couple of times."

"Why were you in China?" I asked, desperately trying to direct the conversation anywhere else.

"I was on a sort of pilgrimage," the friend offered quietly.

The other man continued, as if he'd never read a room in his life. "She also slept with not one, but two of his friends. Not me of course," he announced, "I'm from out of town. Speaking of which, I've got a plane to catch, so if we could get the cheque that would be great."

He paid and left.

"Do you want another beer?" I asked the remaining man, trying to diffuse the awkwardness that had settled over us. "It's on me."

"Nah," he replied, "I should go to the gym, try to keep my spirits up and all that. You're a nice kid. Thanks for the good service."

When my shift ended, I rushed home, speeding to make it through the lights. I knew I had to quit the job before it got deeper into me. I prayed I still had a partner to come home to, though I wouldn't have questioned such a thing mere months before.

I found a job at a diner where I could wear jeans and enormous T-shirts and forget about my body underneath. Initially, the woman who ran the place struck me as kind. But I had never been very good at reading people.

In the four months I lasted, seven people quit and four were fired. Whenever I showed up to open the restaurant, there was usually at least one unfamiliar face in the kitchen. The stranger and I would engage in a standoff until we were sure the other person hadn't just wandered in off the street. An unhoused man had once found his way into the basement's dry storage room (where someone later discovered him sleeping on the paper towels), so it wasn't a completely implausible suspicion.

I never got used to the employee disappearances. Staff would be scheduled, then vanish. I didn't have to look far for the reason. On any given Saturday night, while in the throes of a three-day drunk, the boss would get mean.

The restaurant wasn't much more than a hallway, the kitchen a closet-sized room at its end. You could hear the boss reaming out one of the cooks in the rear, while you served a table up front.

"Could I get you another drink?" I'd ask my customers, who'd heard her every word, and couldn't wait to get out of there.

Later, I'd watch her, half-in-the-bag and sailing around the room. A middle-aged couple once interrupted her trajectory to ask, "Why is the coffee so good?"

"Because" she answered, shakily pouring the molten liquid into their cups, "we brew it with rage."

When I arrived at 10:00 a.m., I'd find the chef out back chain-smoking, already fuming about the day's injustices. Once, I turned up to discover a student crew filming inside the restaurant. None of us had been told about it. The chef and I stood out back, unable to ready ourselves for the morning rush because a woman in too-tight red pants kept admonishing us for ruining each take.

When at last the troupe made their exit, I had to stop the woman in the red pants from stealing my travel mug—still hot with that morning's coffee.

"I thought it was a prop," she claimed.

"Did you really though?" I fired back, as I snatched it from her hand.

The film crew's attraction to the space was warranted. When the bowling alley next door closed, the boss bought up its turquoise Formica countertops and the kitsch hanging over the lanes. Because of its size and shape, the restaurant looked like a single lane. Sometimes, the boss got drunk enough to break out her set of ten-pins after we closed for the night, guttering her big blue bowling ball between the legs of the tables.

Before working at that restaurant, I'd often eaten there, digging the out-of-order, sticky-fronted jukeboxes that topped each table. But the glamour had long since worn off. The first time I'd been given the mop I was told, "Just make the dirt look even."

The boss picked off employees slowly, wearing their confidence down until they either quit or she got around to firing them. Her ex had taken off with one of the waitresses more than a decade before and she'd been punishing every female in her orbit ever since. I watched her pick on the girl she'd hired before me and when that girl was gone, it was my turn.

On the first of a string of bad nights, I stood at the till, taking payment from a table of customers. We were trying to ignore my boss. She sat at the bar top directly to my right, drunkenly pelting me with gummy bears.

"The problem is that you don't move fast enough," Lyla, one of the other servers, advised as we sat rolling cutlery. "Of course, you're also the only person who works in the front of house and doesn't do cocaine."

I knew by then that most of my coworkers had drug habits. Some merely dabbled. For others, the lunch rush came, and with it the bump that got you through the chaos. The restaurant was also one of the last holdouts for drinking on shift. In most establishments, long gone were the days when I watched coworkers drunkenly drop trays and, in one case, literally pass out on top of a table they were serving. But here, there was tequila all the time. When I was still new, this was sort of fun. I flitted around the edges, accepting the occasional shot and wondering how my coworkers could work with all that liquor in their systems.

"It's the cocaine," Lyla explained, "it tempers the booze. Do you not know anything about this drug?"

I admitted, while cocaine had been around me for years, I'd seen what it did to my friends and their bank accounts and refused to touch the stuff. I also knew by then how I did drugs. I was afraid I'd like it, and that I'd never stop. Instead, I preferred to split a handful of mushrooms with someone and get lost in my own neighbourhood.

"You should think about doing a little coke," Lyla suggested.

"To advance my career?" I joked.

"No. So you can keep it."

The diner served a dessert called Bananas Foster which contained rum, butter, bananas, and sugar. We fixed it in front of our tables atop a rickety serving cart with a little burner that folded neatly into a suitcase. You threw all the ingredients together and then you set them on fire.

The first time I'd been tasked with making it, the reedy Viking-looking guy who'd withstood the boss' wrath the longest cautioned me, "Be careful with this, eh? I once burned off the bottom five inches of my beard when I set it alight."

I prepared the dessert but left the gas on when I went to the kitchen for ice cream. I had stopped sleeping on the nights before my shifts, and I guess that's why I didn't notice flames shooting towards the ceiling when I walked away. The boss came out of her office before any of the tiles caught fire, but the reprimand I received was scathing anyway. I slunk back into the kitchen to finish my side duties when she was done.

The chef on duty followed me into the tiny walk-in and asked, "Why are you putting up with this? You're pretty. You could work anywhere."

"Why does that even matter?" I huffed, as he bent down to grab a tray of butter and I flattened myself against the rear wall of the cooler.

"You know how this job works," he reminded me gently. "If you don't like it, find something else."

He was right of course, and when he didn't turn up a few days later, I wasn't surprised. By then, the clanking of the buckles on my boss' boots sounded like spurs when she stalked me through the narrow alley of the restaurant. Her complaints were now about the smallest things: the way I lifted a coffee cup to refill it and how loudly I rolled cutlery. I knew her only reason for keeping me was that she was short-staffed. When I did quit, it was without fanfare. The boss had begun to space my shifts so far out that they looked like mistakes on the schedule.

"I don't think this is working out," I told her and, for once, she didn't disagree with me.

After my last shift, I popped into another bar—a place I'd also worked for a time—and sat facing the wall of windows on one side of the building. The surface of the painted concrete outside became slick in the ice and the snow and I'd sometimes seen people fall, flinging shopping bags and takeout containers in all directions.

One of my old managers slid into the booth across from me, interrupting my revery with a pair of shots. "If you'd have let me know you were going to work for that woman," she declared, as we clinked the little glasses together, "I'd have told you not to."

I moved on again; aware I was running out of places to go. I'd seen others like me, people who'd made the rounds of every bar in our small city, finally taking jobs they didn't want at the last places that would have them.

At the new gig, I went through the motions. I learned the menu and the names of my coworkers. Some were older than me. Those in their teens and twenties were foal-like and wore identical sets of enormous false lashes. The glue on these curling monstrosities would melt if my coworkers got too close to the heaters on the kitchen line, fusing their eyeballs shut. I spent a portion of my shifts handing off their food as they stood a safe distance away.

I tried to flee the bar as early as I could, not wanting to navigate the nearby neighbourhood in the dark when I walked to my car. Staff would be towed if they used the building's parking lot. But one night I broke my habit and stayed late to drink a glass of wine with the owner, Tony. I told him about the man I'd just served who'd suggested the debit machine wasn't working because all the metal in my face was interfering with its connection.

"People can't talk to you like that," Tony assured me. "Why didn't you come and get me?"

"Because I didn't want to hide behind you," I admitted, unsure of how to take this kindness. I jutted my chin out defiantly at him, as if I expected him to hit me. He didn't of course, only comped my drink and told me to have a good night.

As I skidded to my car on icy sidewalks, I thought of what Tony had said and that maybe not every boss in the industry was bad news. Above me, the flickering streetlights blinked bright and then went out for good.

A few days later, while I was changing a keg, one of the managers joined me in the walk-in cooler. This space was much roomier than it had been at my last gig, and she lounged comfortably on a stack of lettuce.

"Tony had a heart attack," she said. "He'll be alright now, though things were pretty touch-and-go at first."

"Holy shit."

"Oh damn," she exclaimed, as I tried to hide my face behind a flat of strawberries. "You're crying."

On a busy night not long after Tony's return from the hospital, I slipped on a patch of wet floor in the kitchen, my feet flying out from underneath me. I landed with one arm flung over my head, my ribs smashing into a stack of serving trays.

On the security camera footage, the trays come shooting out underneath me—pure slapstick. It looks like I've struck my skull on a nearby post, though I was lucky enough to narrowly miss it. Most of the bar's regular customers saw this footage after the manager on duty that night posted it online. I held my side as I did my cash-out, the gasps of near-strangers like a soundtrack behind me as the video circulated through my workplace.

When I still couldn't raise my arm over my head a week afterward, I went to see a doctor. The bar tried to refuse my claim for Workers' Compensation. How could I be sure, they wanted to know, that I'd sustained the injury on the job? It was a good thing then, that I had hundreds of witnesses and video evidence. I took a few days off and returned with ribs stained vivid chartreuse.

"If you really hurt yourself so badly in the fall, why didn't you file the paperwork right away?" Tony wanted to know.

"Because I didn't want to be any trouble," I told him. "I was hoping the pain would go away on its own."

"You don't know how much this costs me," he groused.

"Sorry," I said, not really feeling sorry at all.

He ignored me.

"Not long ago, a couple of the cooks were having a knife-throwing competition. One of them put a blade through the other's hand. Guess who had to pay for the rehab?"

"I wasn't goofing off," I reminded him.

I darted away, hoping that would be the end of it. But he was more intent on getting his pound of flesh than I realized.

Days later, I stood in front of the computer putting in orders. I had my back to the room and didn't see Tony come up behind me. But I did feel the fleshy flat of his hand as he thrust it deep into the rear-crevice of my pants and ran it up the length of my ass.

I whirled around, agog. He stood there, grinning at me.

"Why would you do that?" I demanded.

"Why wouldn't I?"

I got a phone call a couple of days later from a woman who'd interviewed me a month before for a union job in the city's public library system.

"Can you start in two weeks?"

"I can."

"Excellent."

"You know," I blurted, "I was sure I wouldn't hear from you."

"Then you should have a little more faith in yourself."

I put in my notice at the bar, thinking that I'd likely moonlight in the industry to keep my hand in it. But I haven't been back since.

"True or not,
I've had worse
reputations."

The Leaving Drawer

I KEEP A DRAWER that's just for leaving. It holds my passport, a few different currencies, and several pairs of underwear. I find it a comfort to know that, at any time, I can heft it from the dresser and escape my life.

I spent much of my twenties living transiently. When I did return to the place I came from, it was only to save up enough money to leave again. I got used to saying goodbye to objects that weighed me down. My rented apartments contained unpacked boxes and had bare white walls. Between trips, I would lay awake thinking about what I would take if I only had my beat-up car to carry my possess ions. It was a hobby that would serve me well when I left a bad relationship in a hurry one afternoon.

Over those years, I crawled through the blackness of water-filled caves, my hands touching the many-legged things that scuttled away from my fingers in the darkness; I fled the crashing bulk of a full-grown male orangutan as he made for my left-behind lunch; I bowled with Vietnamese businessmen, the lanes somehow exempt from the city-wide curfew, and had to walk back to my hotel afterwards down poorly-lit streets in the company of strangers—the cab services all shut down for the night.

I thought I was afraid I might miss something in the parts of the world I hadn't yet visited. But, in truth, I was afraid if I set my backpack down long enough, I might never pick it up again. And it was that fear that kept me moving.

Over the last few years, I've been trying to learn how to settle into a life. I've made friends, good friends, and the ones I had before I'm closer to. I've also moved in with someone who owns a house and can't leave at a moment's notice.

The first time I visited his place, I was surprised to see that he cultivated roses. In the beds out front, he had big scarlet Emily Carr roses, tiny blush-pink tea roses, and vivid Ketchup & Mustard roses—though I couldn't have named any of them then. As he gazed benevolently down at his flowers, he told me their care had seriously injured him once. He'd been trying to remove a dead rosebush with a hatchet. The plant had slipped out of his fingers just as he brought the blade down, and he'd smashed it into his left arm. "I thought I'd cut a tendon," he recounted, "but I'd actually broken a bone."

This moment of violence aside, the roses reflected a softness I didn't expect in this man who left engine oil handprints on my white apartment walls. Before we lived together, I would find rose blooms tucked underneath the windshield wipers of my car like a fragrant note saying he'd been nearby at some point during the day.

The places I'd lived before had sometimes included patchy extensions of scrub-grass filled with bottles and trash. But the yard at his house was meticulously cared for. Alone in this new place, I would walk barefoot over the thick grass, the newly seeded spots I'd been forbidden to tread on feeling particularly decadent beneath my toes. I got into the habit of sitting out on the back deck at sunset and imagining a garden.

My friend Alice encouraged me to give it a try (though after clearing the last of my personal effects from her garage, she was perhaps more invested than most in my staying put). Produce crawled across her lawn in thick, coiling sheets of green. She grew pumpkins the size of human torsos; dill as tall as my thigh; and kale so heavy with aphids that when she passed some along to me, it came with the suggestion that I run it through a quick spin cycle in my washing machine before eating it. Alice seemed to me a sort of earth goddess who might have birds carry her to work, if only she would ask them to.

She got one of a handful of permits in a pilot project to house chickens within city limits. Each time I visited her, chickens trotted through the yard, pecking at the vast garden. Not too far off, the sound of a city bus could be heard, breaking for the stop on the corner, before heading to the nearby mall so large it could be seen from space.

Things went well with the flock until Alice's chicken mentor suggested she adopt a rescued hen. The stray infected its new brethren with an incurable respiratory illness. But Alice couldn't bring herself to wring the necks of her chickens, many of whom had been named for her great aunts. "Did you know you can just put their carcasses out with your regular garbage?" she grappled. "You just have to double bag them. Doesn't that seem wildly insensitive to you? I mean, it's not as if they're shampoo bottles."

I agreed it did seem a careless way to dispose of a dead animal. We were standing in her basement at the time, and suddenly something darted around the corner.

"Was that a chicken in a diaper?" I asked.

"It was. Did you know there's such a thing as chicken diapers?"

"I did not. But that's not the part of this that I'm really hung up on."

"That chicken is sicker than the rest, and the others are picking on her. So, I brought her inside. The poor gal's vagina is falling out," Alice explained.

"The whole thing?" I asked, stunned, and then, thinking better of it, halted her mid-answer, "you know what, never mind. I don't need to know."

"That's probably best."

Having decided to change the topic, I nodded in the direction of Alice's esthetics station and asked, "But what do you do with her when you have clients?"

"I just keep her down here. She's quiet."

"So, you mean to tell me that she could walk in at any moment?"

"Yep."

I imagined that: a woman's legs splayed open for a bikini wax, when suddenly a chicken in a diaper wandered in. It sounded like the beginning of a bad joke.

"Seems risky."

She shrugged off the comment and asked, "Did I tell you I'm thinking of keeping bees?"

I worried that Alice's progression was common, that I'd plant a couple of carrots and, not long afterward, I'd have a goat living in my spare room that I was claiming as a dependant on my taxes.

Ignoring my reservations, Alice began to bring me cuttings of her hardiest house plants: a spider plant that soon became plump with babies; a purple heart that turned from soft green to the rich, dark colour of red cabbage when left in the sun.

A few months into this parade of plants, Alice swung by carrying a planter filled with monkshood, though I didn't know enough to recognize its cowl-shaped purple flowers.

"Guess what this perennial is?"

I blinked back at her.

"I'll give you a hint: don't eat it."

This was particularly ironic. Some weeks before, I'd inherited a Swedish ivy plant from a cousin who'd insisted it was basil mint. "I don't think it's edible," I'd told Alice, fingering the strange leaves. When I turned my back to her, I heard her chewing.

Meanwhile, my partner—who'd only just stopped asking whether I was going to unpack the last of my boxes and had moved them to the basement—built me a garden for my birthday. The small wooden rectangle was already filled with plants. He'd put in an automatic watering system too in case I forgot about it. I watched the garden grow, the tendrils of squash slipping out of the box and spreading themselves across the lawn. To me, the produce that developed on its vines seemed curvaceous, sexual almost, the curve of the acorn squash reminding me of the bowl of a woman's hips. The gourds flattened the grass beneath them, and the vines anchored themselves every few feet, like fingers digging into the dirt.

Not long before it was time to harvest the garden, a familiar wave of panic set in and stayed. Almost without thinking, I opened my leaving drawer, booked a plane ticket, and flew to Stockholm. I spent a month and a half galivanting around Europe, while my partner cultivated the garden alone.

While I was in Sweden, he sent pictures of enormous dark green zucchinis more closely resembling weapons than fruit. When I moved on to Germany, he sent evidence of fat, yellow spaghetti squash, their skins in the sun the colour of spun gold. By the time I landed in Poland, he'd moved on to sending photos of heavy branches of cherry tomatoes, so laden with fruit he couldn't eat them all before they rotted. By the time I came home the squash was diced and frozen. Out back, all that remained of the garden was a solitary patch of black dirt. I had missed it.

The following year, I promised myself I would stay put. My partner and I bought too many plants for our little patch and had to fill carefully scrubbed hydraulic oil pails with dirt. The peas and tomatoes didn't seem to mind. They grew to the height of my armpits, the tomatoes jewel-like beneath the blazing summer sun, the peas fat, green crescent-moons.

I waited, a bit impatiently, for the squash to come. Under my eye, the vines grew, and the flowers bloomed, but no gourds developed. When I asked Alice why this might be, she suggested that perhaps we didn't have any bees in the area. I would have to pollinate the female flowers myself.

"How do I do that?"

"Well, first, you pour them a nice glass of red wine, then you put on some Barry White, then you run a hot bath..."

"You're hilarious."

"Aren't I though?"

Despite my pollinating efforts, the squash never did come that year. Perhaps it was just too wet for them.

When spring arrived the following year, I dug in my heels against the pull of elsewhere. My partner and I bought a grow light and started seedlings. We studied the *Farmer's Almanac*, trying to divine when the last winter frost might come in our unpredictable northern climate. We waited, shuttling our seedlings in and out of the house on cookie sheets, hardening them off.

I studied our neighbours' properties for clues. Most planted early and had to spread blankets over their crops in the evenings, as if tucking in children who'd insisted on sleeping outside. We followed suit, planting kale and peas, those heartier garden denizens. A couple weeks later, we put in the more delicate things and were delighted when each familiar green sprout reached for the sun.

In that same sky, planes flew overhead. I watched them, waiting for the familiar pang of panic to flare because I was not on one of them. But it never did come.

The Gospels of Warning

While having brunch with a girlfriend who works as a nurse, she tells me, "You wouldn't be able to get an abortion if you wanted one right now."

We are well into the pandemic at this point, our masks folded beside us on the table like elaborate napkins. I play with the ear loops of mine while I listen.

"Elective procedures are paused, and abortions could be considered elective. If you really don't want to have a child, now's the time to be cautious."

"I am being cautious," I lie.

"No," she quips, spearing a potato for emphasis, "you're not."

Over the tedious months of the pandemic, I watch the women around me round at the waist with increasing frequency. They waddle past in pairs, nautical stripes stretched tight over their bellies. Some wear matching sweatsuits, the tops riding up to show the protruding punctuation mark of their navels and the dark line bisecting their stomachs, as if a shadowy thing lives inside of them. In an epidemic, this reads as its own sort of contagion.

As a library worker, I am more exposed than most to the baby parade. I spend my days with my hand stuffed into a ferret puppet or leading a dozen sets of tiny sneakers on a scavenger hunt, a cape of children trailing after me.

At the end of my shifts, I drive home with pockets stuffed full of book call numbers and mismatched googly eyes. I blast The Cramps to scrub my brain of the earworm that is Sticky Sticky Bubblegum.

As the highway unfurls, the blacktop waved with frost heaves, I think of my mother's maiden name. The direct translation of the Cyrillic characters is "rattle." Of all the dictionary definitions, it is not tied to the one that means: *to alarm or fluster*. Instead, it refers to an instrument or plaything crafted to make noise, especially that given to babies. I interpret this word, this thing I am linked to by blood, as a warning knell.

At last, I book an appointment to see my doctor. When she shuffles into the exam room, I am shocked to see that she is hugely pregnant. At just over five feet tall and perhaps a hundred pounds, she looks cartoonish—like a woman trying to steal the thing stuffed beneath her crisp ecru dress.

"We'll have to use the big exam room at the back, because I can't fit between the bed and the wall in any of the others."

"It looks like congratulations are in order," I fumble.

She grunts in response.

In the quiet of the rear exam room, I let my feet dangle off the table as she sets up for my overdue internal exam. Into the blazing brightness of the fluorescent tube above I ask, "I'm worried about getting pregnant right now, could we talk about that today, too?"

"Of course."

I hear the snap of a speculum clicking open. "What about hormonal birth control pills?"

"They made me crazy, remember? We tried them before."

I have been seeing this knife-blade of a woman for a long time. When she first prescribed hormonal birth control pills, the excess estrogen seemed to bore straight into my brain. I was a house with all the lights on at night, and those driving by could see the woman inside writhing on the floor.

I also didn't trust the pills to be effective. I was then with a man I wasn't sure I wanted to spend my life with, living for part of the year in a country where abortions were illegal. The women there had shrugged at this. If worst came to worst, they assured me, you could always nip over to Cambodia for the procedure; as long as you were less than twelve weeks along, of course.

While there, I picked up a hobby of taking pregnancy tests. In that place (with its huge house lizards that would come back no matter how far out of town you dropped them), I had to build my own tests out of beakers and strips and complicated reams of instructions. These science experiments dotted the countertops of the guest houses I stayed in, while an ever-constant line of marching ants was reflected in the mirror on the wall behind me. They were oblivious to my blind panic as I willed the strip not to turn pink. I can still recall the packaging of one of these tests: a bright pink box with the less than reassuring brand name *Pretty Sure.*

"What about the hormonal IUD?" my doctor suggests.

She is pinned between the wall and the exam table, and a careful dance is done around the stirrups that hold my feet each time she reaches for an instrument. There is a grace to her that I hadn't noticed before the pregnancy. I squirm a little, my butt having gone numb from being perched so long at the edge of the table. I feel as if she is trying to determine my future by reading the inside of me. And in a way, I suppose that's true.

"I had the copper IUD for a while, and that was a bust. I was never not bleeding."

"The hormonal version will be totally different. You'll see. It might even improve your day-to-day. Some women report an end to their periods on it."

"Okay. I'll give it a shot."

A month or so after that visit, I find myself back in the clinic beneath a paper sheet, waiting for the doctor. From the hallway, I can hear the familiar music of Stromae and the tittering of the girls at the front desk speaking French.

Alone in the room, I can't help but think back to my first IUD insertion. It had happened in one of the city's abortion clinics. They did insertions until noon on Mondays, and abortions the rest of the week. The clinic was a grey concrete structure of brutalist design. Just across the street, in a little house with a riotous flower garden of peonies and zinnias, hummed the Prolife Centre. During the required interview before my insertion, the woman opposite me asked if I had gone to the house across the street first.

"You know I'm not here for an abortion, right?"

"I have to ask everyone the same questions," she said, the exhaustion clear in her voice.

After the interview, I was shuffled down a dark hallway under flickering lights. Deeper and deeper into the building I went, as if striding into a cave. At last, I came to a room with lockers where I was told to undress below the waist. I was given a floral blanket to cover myself. In an adjoining room filled with puzzles no one touched, I found a collection of women dressed just as I was. All of us had locker keys pinned to our chests, as if we belonged poolside.

"It's not really so bad," the older women assured those of us doing this for the first time. "You'll see."

By then, it was after noon. Some of us had boxes on our laps, and some of us didn't. Those who didn't kept to themselves. One by one, we were shuffled into yet another room. There, a thin, fatigued woman shone a light into my eyes. A metal rod, like something you'd use to jimmy the lock on a car, disappeared into me.

"It's for measurement," the doctor assured me and, to my relief, pulled it out again.

Afterwards, the attending nurse handed me a mesh ball of what she called "sexy panties." I stuffed them into the pocket of my hoodie and forgot about them. When I did laundry a few days later, they dissolved into fine white threads that coated my clothes.

In the clinic in the French neighbourhood of my city, I think what a blessing it is not to have to return to that dark little center. Here, there is light all around me. A doctor I don't know is doing the IUD insertion. Her face is hidden behind the mist of her breath on the face shield she wears. While my own doctor is on maternity leave, this one has agreed to tend to me.

On the table, I don't move and hardly breathe. There is only a slight pinch, and that is all. It is nothing compared to the insertion of my first IUD. I've heard that once that part of you is opened by something, it stays that way.

"Are you alright?" the assisting nurse asks, peering into my face.

"Perfect."

To keep the IUD sterile, I have not opened its box. If all goes well, I will carry this mysterious thing with me until it is time to change it out five years from now.

I experience two weeks of bleeding. For me, this is nothing new. An old boyfriend once told me, "I've never been with anyone who bleeds as much as you do." And for a second, I'd taken the words as a compliment.

The real problem is the pain, which sometimes makes my legs give out. At work, I find myself grabbing desktops and tables to steady myself. The doctor who did the insertion had claimed it would take about forty-eight hours for the ache to go away. Now I learn that for some women it can take months. I tell myself to give it a year.

Soon, cystic acne begins its slow, spreading bloom across my face. My doctor prescribes antibiotics and topical creams, both of which make me more susceptible to sun damage. No matter the time of day, I coat myself in sunscreen and will only venture outdoors beneath the brim of a huge hat. My skin feels slick and waterproof, as if I am becoming amphibious.

"How could you possibly resist me?" I joke with my partner.

Fat welts bubble up under my skin and surface in a red mass of sores. I look in the mirror and think of the planet Mars.

"I can't," he replies, and kisses me all over my face.

By now, the pain is a constant. With the copper IUD, I'd coped by taking a cocktail of over-the-counter pain killers. Pharmacies in the countries where I was living would give you whatever you wanted, if only you'd ask. While on a ship crossing a grey and tempestuous sea, the other passengers had panicked around me. They raced from one side of the deck to the other, as if things might be better starboard. I watched them with the fingers of one hand curled loosely around a post. By then, I'd given up on dosages and the advice of medical professionals, the IUD like a thing that was trying to claw its way out. I felt the rise and swell of the pitching waves beneath me. Talk of capsizing rippled through the crowd of passengers, but under the haze of medication I couldn't feel a thing. Not even fear.

My current doctor suggests perhaps the IUD has shifted, and that's what's causing all this hurt. I agree to an ultrasound.

At the appointment, I strip down in a cubicle and pull a medical gown over myself. Unable to find any ties, I clutch the back of the gown closed and follow a small woman into a tiny, dark room. The woman gestures to a bed in the corner. I do my best to follow her instruction, but scarcely fit. My head is snugged up to one wall and my feet are flat against the other. She smears cool jelly on my stomach and begins to skate a wand across the slick surface of my abdomen. The dark cavern at the core of me appears on the screen.

"Everything looks good," the woman declares, stepping back. "Now for the internal portion of the exam."

"What do you mean by, 'internal portion?' Isn't this all internal?"

The woman ignores me and produces a different wand. I remember to mention my latex allergy only when she gives me a condom to roll over it. I am presented with a consent form and told, basically, to fuck myself.

"It might hurt a little."

I almost laugh at her choice of words. Right now, everything hurts a little.

I do what I am told, while the tech looks politely away. It is an odd time for decorum. Again, my interior blinks up on the screen. This time, the view is a more intimate one.

"It's good you're skinny. That makes it easier to see everything."

Sure enough, the screen shows some of the vertebrae of my spine. They seem to glow like streetlights on a dark night. The tech takes photo after photo as I do my best to keep still.

"Smile," she jokes, but I can't quite manage it.

Soon, I hear from my temporary doctor. The IUD is perfectly in place. The failing then, is my own. Only six months have gone by with it in, and I decide to keep holding out. I remind myself that with the copper IUD, I bled with such furious suddenness I ruined car seats. And, after a while, no cocktail of painkillers could dull even the edges of my hurt.

I think back to the time I stood in a field of tall grass in Gippsland, Australia. My then-boyfriend's father was eager to show me how his beagle herded kangaroos. The dog barked and a mob of the huge animals swept across the paddock in a flood of reddish-brown fur, their powerful legs rocketing them high into the air. I was simultaneously wowed and incapacitated. I stood, half-bent at the waist, fighting to keep my head high enough to see.

In Australia, the doctors I saw would not remove that first IUD without a negative STI screening. After a false positive for one of the particularly scary ones, another string of tests was needed. By the time I was negative for certain, my visa was near its expiry date. I flew home and had the removal done there.

My current suffering does not touch the way I felt back then. But there is pain when I run, when I do yoga, when I work, when I sleep, when I have sex. Something too, is poking my partner during the latter. He and I speculate that the IUD doesn't do anything but hurt. It doesn't need to. My desire, which has always been a constant, is gone.

I mourn this loss of want, as I watch the person I love move through the house where we have lived together for over half a decade. He is the same man, with the same black hair and the dimple that is deeper in one cheek when he smiles. Despite my loss, I still feel our love like a third beating heart in the narrow space between our bodies when we hug. I grab at it, but by the time we pull away it's already gone.

More months pass. Everything stays the same. Then one day I stroll past a windowpane. Reflected in it, I notice a bulge of something on the inside of my left leg. Below my knee there is a green coiling mass: a slender snake beneath the skin. A few inches below that, another little nub pokes out. It is all (I learn from the specialist I see soon after) part of the same incompetent vein.

Progesterone, which is what my IUD is slowly distributing through my body, thins the veins. This is not an issue for those with no prior problems, only for those like me with pre-existing conditions. For years, I've had tightness and pain in my legs after a long shift, yet this is the first time one of my veins has pushed up to the surface.

When I first meet the specialist, he strides into the room and looks me up and down. I am wearing shorts because I was told to.

"I can't believe it's my job to look at legs all day," he comments.

I push down my discomfort and inquire about laser removal and sugar-water injections. He gives me a bemused smile. This problem is past those solutions. Instead, he will be making several incisions in my skin and pulling out the vein and its dead branches with a hook. After that, the blood will reroute itself and new veins will grow.

"And then?"

"And then we'll see each other as much as you think necessary. Varicose veins are a recurring problem."

By now, eleven months have passed since the IUD's insertion. That, I decide, is long enough to declare the experiment a failure. The familiar black boxes of latex-free condoms begin to call to me as I saunter through the aisles of my neighbourhood pharmacy.

When I return to my usual clinic, my doctor is back from maternity leave. I am elated to see her delicate, fox-like face. Even the twitch of disapproval at the corner of her mouth, when I tell her how much I've been drinking, is a welcome familiarity.

I list off the side effects I'm experiencing because of the device implanted in me. I admit I haven't slept a full night in the two weeks preceding this appointment. I don't tell her about my obsession with the main character of the dystopian novel *Blue Ticket*, a woman who yanked out her own IUD with pliers.

My doctor leans towards me, her face kind. "Do you just want me to take it out?"

"Could you?" I ask, and realize I am near tears.

"Of course. Just let me set up."

I undress as she goes out to collect the necessary tools. Then, I am laying back on the examination table.

"Make a buzzing noise."

I give her a funny look.

"Like a bee. I find the vibrations help with the removal."

I follow her instruction until there is a painful yank. Making like a bee doesn't really help. It only distracts enough so you can't predict when the pain is coming, like someone pulling a tooth on the count of two when they promised they'd wait until three.

"That's it," she says, and holds up the IUD to the light like an archeological find.

This white, anchor-shaped piece of plastic is bigger than I thought it would be. The top of the T is nearly three centimetres wide, with a stem that's slightly longer. The strings, used to check if the device is in place, measure just over eight centimetres and resemble brilliant blue fishing line.

"Can I keep it?"

There is a long pause before my doctor agrees.

When I get home, I'm not sure what to do with it. It's too big for a ring box. In the end, I fold up a little pink origami boat and drop the IUD onto its deck. Then, I wait to feel like myself again..

Within days, the pain recedes. A crushing fatigue floods into the space it leaves behind. Like a bear woken in winter, I want to sleep and sleep and sleep. I had been warned about the progesterone crash that might come with the IUD's removal. But when I searched online, most of the links led to personal injury lawyers.

To shake the fatigue from my limbs, I meet up with a girlfriend to bike through the southern hills of the city. As soon as we set out, the sky opens on us in blinding sheets of rain. We decide to keep going, and the day clears. Over and over again, we get lost, as is our habit. The ride stretches on. When we reach the crest of a steep hill, I am still waiting for the pain to come, for my body to seize around the lightning rod inside of me. But it doesn't. There is only the delicious burn in my thighs and the yoke-yellow sun in the sky as the light at its edges turns a crepuscular purple.

Some weeks afterwards, I sit at the kitchen island watching my partner. He is looking for something in the refrigerator. "To your left," I coach. "No, your other left."

I realize, in this purely mundane moment, as he stands inside the glowing maw of the fridge, that I want him. And that everything is going to be alright.

A Cauldron of Bats

In early April 2021, I found myself on the way to a writer's residency in Western Canada. My destination was nearly seven-hundred kilometres away in another province. This being in the thick of the pandemic, I was prepared to quarantine for my first fourteen days. Cans of chickpeas and jars of dried lentils rattled in my back seat each time I hit a pothole.

As I drove, I noted the ponds were still ice-covered, though the geese had already returned. The birds must have known how precariously frozen these bodies of water were, because they trod carefully across their surfaces, like women in high heels mincing along icy sidewalks.

Outside the town of Czar, where (according to the town sign) cowboys reigned, I spotted a wolf. I'd always pictured them just a little bigger than coyotes but saw I'd been wrong about that. The thing outside my car was a monster. I thought about pulling over to take photos but caught myself. This was a predator, and I was a girl alone in a Corolla.

A few hours into the trip, the wind reached a deafening crescendo. It felt like I was carrying a fitful passenger along with me and, every so often, this person would reach over and wrench the wheel from my hands. I kept flipping on my little tape recorder to make notes. Later, when I played them back, I could hear the wind howling in the background, persistent as an irate poltergeist. In the recording, I note I've started to see gophers everywhere and I say a prayer I won't hit one. The tape goes blank and a few seconds later switches on again so my frantic voice can admit to killing one.

By the time I reached the residency in early evening, my upper arms were sore from gripping the wheel. The house looked exactly the way it had in the pictures, with four gables, a windowed-in front porch, and an office that overlooked grass-topped hills at the rear. Outside, everything was still dry and brown. Tumbleweeds skittered past, quick and fleeting as ghosts.

The first days were a blur of work. The author who'd lived in the house as a boy wrote about his plans to haunt the house after death, and I had to admit the structure didn't feel empty. The roof needed to be replaced, and when the wind blew, it sounded like someone was walking across the ancient cedar shingles. Still, I did my best to dissolve into the pages I'd written, glancing up only when the sun began to set in the office window, turning the sky dusky purple. Everything was nearly perfect, but for the small squirming bug I found on the desktop the first night, and the spray of what looked like red paint coating the tops of the office walls.

In the evenings, I sat on the porch and thought about how familiar this part of the country felt to me. My parents had been born in this province, and my brother and I were sometimes left at our maternal grandparents' farm here in the summers. We would grow feral as the days stretched on, our skins sun-darkened and too dirty for quick recognition when our parents came to collect us. I still remember the sight of bats swarming out of the barn when my Gido flung the doors open to the twilight.

I also carry a burned-in image of tire-flattened, turquoise-bellied salamanders, their bodies pancaked on the road, as I stood nearby with my thumb out, hoping some farmer might stop and ferry me into town for ice cream. My brother and I only had each other to play with during those months. Yet we could go entire days without seeing each other. Often, he was away shooting gophers. I sometimes discovered their torn-off tails stuffed in the pockets of the coats he had borrowed.

When paging through the house's guestbook, I discovered I knew the woman who had stayed a couple of months before me. The two of us had met at a writer's retreat in

Saskatchewan, the same province I now found myself in. She was a talented singer, but that's not what I remembered most about her. Instead, it was her speech during our introductory meet-and-greet. She warned us of the ticks in the area, and how some of them now carried Lyme disease. She advised us to shake out our clothing and give our naked bodies a good looking over after our walks.

"You are all beautiful," she had murmured, in the benevolent tone of a saint.

After my walks in this new place, I still heeded her advice. I stripped down and shook out my clothes in the bathtub. Naked before the mirror, I inspected the folds of my labia and the backs of my knees. I heard her voice as I bent over, and knew it was perhaps not the legacy she'd hoped for.

When I went to put my jeans back on after this ritual one night, I noticed a little red bug crawling across the floor. It seemed too small to be a tick, but I caught it in a tissue and flushed it anyway.

The following night, I saw two of the same bugs on the mat beside my bed. I shook them out into the tub, and something niggled at me. About a decade before, while backpacking through Cambodia with my ex, we discovered our hotel room was teeming with bedbugs. I had a stomach parasite and was too sick to leave the bathroom, let alone move hotels. We talked about calling an ambulance, but I thought I could wait it out. He bought some large white antibiotic pills in a pharmacy, and I managed to keep them down. As soon as we could, we fled the hotel.

Alone in the idyllic bedroom in the retreat house on the prairies, I brought up a picture of a bedbug on my phone, and there were the little red demons. After riffling through the bedclothes, I didn't find any more. But out in the hallway, I looked up. There, in the clear plastic that sealed the drafty attic was a swarm of the bugs: small and red like skittering apple seeds. The plastic had come undone. Knowing it was futile; I pressed it closed. That night, I hardly slept at all.

In the morning, I called the coordinator. "I've noticed these little red bugs everywhere," I explained as calmly as I could.

"Yes," she said nonchalantly, "they're bat bugs."

"Oh," I sputtered, instantly relieved, "I was sure they were bedbugs."

"No. They look very similar though. We had bats in the attic. They were relocated two years ago. We're just waiting for the bugs to die. They're not interested in you, it's the bats they want."

"I see."

I hung up the phone and relaxed for a few minutes. But never one to leave well enough alone, I dialed a pest control company.

"Hello," I greeted the stranger on the other end of the line. "I've just found out I'm living in a house with bat bugs."

"Oh dear."

"The bats that carried the bugs in have been relocated." I pressed on, "but I'm wondering what to expect now."

"If bat bugs are deprived of their preferred food source, they'll begin to behave like their cousins, bedbugs. They'll turn to whatever's available for a blood meal."

"So, that would be me, right?"

"I mean…yeah."

"I've found just a few in the house." I relayed, trying to keep the panic out of my voice. "Is it possible that's the end of them?"

"They're prolific egg-layers, so I really doubt it."

The tranquil office seemed to dissolve around me. In its place, I could only see the blood-spatter lining the top of the walls. This, I learned, from the same phone call, was a telltale sign of the bugs feeding on sculptors and writers and painters. Oh my.

I slept even less that night. My first inclination was to leave, but I'd made a commitment. It was not lost on me that the residency had been pushed back due to the Covid-19 pandemic, once thought to have been brought on by contact between humans and bats. And here I sat, quarantined in a house where I was being nibbled by their parasites too. What was perhaps even more ironic, was that the book I was supposed to be working on had a character who coughed up bats.

In Slavic folklore, there is a figure named Koshchei the Deathless. Koshchei's death exists on the head of a pin, inside an egg, inside a bird, and sometimes that bird is inside a rabbit too. The animal containing the egg is often on a faraway island or buried beneath a remote tree. Koshchei cannot be killed until the egg is found by the hero of the story—a figure who usually wants the hand of the princess Koshchei is keeping captive. In all the folklore I'd read, the clever princess had either learned the egg's whereabouts, or the prince who loved her had coaxed it out of Koshchei, and the deathless man was now dead.

In my version of the story, Koshchei's death was in the belly of a lost bird, and he had gone on to live a Methuselah-like lifespan. The bats he expelled were a side effect of his extended years. I'd spent months researching their species for the book. I'd learned the Vesper, or evening bat, had the largest family, with four-hundred-eighty-five species, that the deciduous or *milk teeth* of baby bats could grip their mother's nipple in flight, and that bats could expel carbon dioxide and take in oxygen from their skin—something they shared with only a select number of very young marsupials. Then there was the name of their taxonomic order: *Chiroptera*, which translated, quite beautifully I thought, to *hand wings*.

While I was researching the book, I could talk of almost nothing else but bats. At a party some months before, the only person I knew was a woman in a silver lamé dress who'd passed out in a chair as soon as we'd arrived. While she slept, I huddled in a corner talking to a man about bats. After an hour or so, the man put a hand on my arm and told me, very earnestly, he was happily married. My fixation on the creatures had read, somehow, as seduction.

Yet, despite all my research, I'd known nothing of bat parasites before arriving at the residency. Sleepless nights on Google taught me bedbugs and bat bugs are blood-sucking insects from the family *Cimicidae.* They're small, oval, and flat if they've not fed. When humans resided in caves, both bat and bedbugs fed on them. When we moved on to other dwellings, bedbugs followed, but bat bugs stayed behind, preferring their winged meals. If you wish to differentiate between the two, the bat bugs have longer hairs on the upper covering of their thorax.

Some members of the residency council sent a few of the bugs away to be examined two years previous, but the confirmation these were bat bugs was as far as anyone had gotten with the problem. No one on the council seemed aware that the bugs preferred to stay above floor level but would move closer to sleeping humans if left without another meal option. The bugs were known to nest in the crevices of mattresses and bedding, as well as woodwork, trim, furniture, drapery pleats, peeling wallpaper, picture frames, and books. Pretty much everywhere. I made myself crazy looking for evidence of them. Behind articles about the famous author, I found more fine, crimson blood spatter, like tiny rectangular crime scenes.

I contacted the singer who'd warned me about ticks to ask if she'd brought any of the bugs home with her. "I never saw a live one while at the residency," she wrote back, "only their dead little husks. But I'll be going through my things feverishly now."

After this brief correspondence, I didn't hear from her again and couldn't say I blamed her. I was the girl with the bugs. I might show up only to open my coat and release a squirming tide of them onto her pristine living room carpet. I wouldn't have returned my emails either.

Perplexed as to why I was the first one to experience problems, I soon got an answer about this from the coordinator.

"The bugs become more active in warmer weather," she told me, during one of our many phone calls. "Their eggs also develop more quickly in the heat." It was the newly balmy temperatures that had brought them out of hiding, and in greater numbers.

While washing the sheets the next day, I found one of the bugs crawling through the bedclothes. I called the coordinator, who finally contacted an exterminator. Because the town the house was in was rather remote, he couldn't come for another two weeks. It was just me and the bugs until then, and I had another full week of quarantine to go. To make matters worse, I was one of those people who didn't show bedbug bites, and it looked to be the same with the bat bugs. Some people developed allergic reactions to proteins injected from the saliva of the bugs. Some suffered welts. Some, like me, showed nothing at all. My only symptom was the fierce, psychosomatic itching. I had no conclusive proof the bugs were feeding on me.

The coordinator and her husband dropped by armed with another temporary barrier method and poison. When they lifted the attic flap to spray the poison, a handful of bugs and a shower of bat guano rained down on our heads. After three days without sleep, I thought it looked like the worst sort of confetti.

After their visit, every paint chip, rice kernel, and speck of dirt aroused my suspicions. I lived in fear. What was more, the caretakers of the house were very intent for me to stay, even after pest control came, a period after which I could expect a temporary increase in activity. I began to spend the nights (the bugs' most active time) walking through the house, armed with a flashlight, searching for parades of insects.

"Whatever you want to do is fine with me," my partner assured me when I called him. "If you want to stay the rest of the month, I'm behind you. If you want to come home tomorrow, that's okay too. As long as you don't bring them home."

"And if I do?"

"If you do, you'll be looking for an apartment."

"A couple of bug bites and it's all over, eh?"

"You'll sleep in the shed for the first month. It'll be fine."

"That doesn't sound fine."

"I promise to run the lawnmower every day, so you'll have something warm to snuggle at night."

I started calling various pest control outfits the way some people called sex lines: frequently and in a panic. I couldn't help myself. I had so many, many questions. I reached out to a woman with a company in Swift Current during a particularly feverish day.

"What's the likelihood I'll bring the bugs home with me?"

I think she could tell I was going crazy, so she was gentle with me.

"As long as you're careful," she soothed, "you should be fine."

"Careful," I repeated, as if there was something cryptic in this word.

"Is there anything else?"

"Yes. What are you wearing?"

"What?"

"Nothing."

This was not what you might think. I only wanted to know if she was dressed in a garbage bag with slits cut out for her arms. If I worked in her industry, I certainly would have been.

When I tried to contact her again, the number went to a voicemail greeting that said nothing about a pest control company. I looked at online maps of the business, and saw it was a house. I wondered if she was just some woman who had put her information up online for people like me, mid-panic, to find. Perhaps she was not even a person at all, but the modern version of a patron saint for the infested. I went online and found that St. Dominic of Silos is the patron saint who guards against insects and rabid dogs. I could not decide if it was significant that he protected pregnant women too.

Each time I opened the freezer, I had to push my purse aside. It had been in the bedroom when I'd found the first two bugs and had been on ice ever since. Though I knew this was pointless. Only extreme heat could kill the bugs. During my research, I'd found one scholarly article that told of bedbugs who reanimated after five years in the freezer.

But then, what to do with all the books I'd brought? As a library assistant, I knew that bedbugs liked to hide out in the spines of books and had heard of a library in Florida that kept a book oven to kill the pests and their eggs. But if I did so, I might start a fire in the hundred-year-old wooden house.

"You don't want the reputation of being the person who burned down that house," a friend told me, when I brought the idea up to him.

"I worked as a bar waitress for over a decade. True or not, I've had worse reputations."

To further test the oven theory, I mentioned my musings to my partner. He, in turn, said nothing.

"I'm seriously thinking of cooking the books," I prompted him a second time.

"Don't put books in the oven."

"I won't."

But I'd already found the fire extinguisher. Really, it was only a matter of time.

Two days after I'd promised I wouldn't, I sat in front of the oven sipping tea. The temperature was set to 170°F, the lowest it would go, while the oven baked several books I'd brought to bed with me. Among them was a copy of

The Empathy Exams by Leslie Jamison. I'd thought I would read while I watched the books. Instead, I stared at them for a whole hour, mesmerized. I had placed a pan of water underneath them, so they wouldn't dry out too much, but still their covers curled a little.

I sipped my tea and thought of the novel, *Fahrenheit 451*, its title a reference to the temperature at which paper supposedly catches fire. Apparently, this number wasn't correct. It was something a firefighter said flippantly to Ray Bradbury once, and the author had taken it as gospel. I wondered if the real temperature was much lower, and I was about to find out for myself in a hundred-year-old house with the closest fire department some thirty-odd kilometres away.

My mind wandered to the essay in *The Empathy Exams* that detailed Morgellons disease. Those who suffered from it saw fibres embedded in their skin. They fished through their flesh, trying to find proof for their doctors. Some brought in matchboxes filled with items they'd dug out of their bodies. Most were diagnosed with delusions. I had no proof the bugs were biting me and, initially, I couldn't even prove they were alive in the house. But I had managed to convince the council there was a problem. I had been believed. I was lucky, so lucky, as I sat in front of an oven, watching to see if the books inside it would burn.

I'd been mostly nude since discovering the bugs. After one had fallen, live and skittering out of a sweater I'd stripped off, I decided to flit about the house without clothes. I was no longer worried the neighbours had seen me naked. I knew they had. Now, it was more a question of for how long, and whether they'd had enough time to take photos. I couldn't help wondering if years down the road, I would see a picture of myself online, a blurry flash as I crossed in front of the upstairs windows in this very house. *Ah, I'd think to myself, I recognize that tattoo, and that ass.*

This nudity reminded me of a friend of my parents' I met once, in Hawaii. He told me a story about the time he'd spent living in Mississippi. Before he'd moved there, the locals had had a habit of vandalizing the property he and his wife bought. But all this stopped when he showed up, loping towards them across the lawn in only a pair of rubber boots.

"It was easier to see the ticks that way," he explained.

As I stood nude in the basement, but for a pair of mukluks, running my few clothes through the cleansing heat of the dryer for the third time that day, I found I understood him completely.

Perhaps upon receiving a complaint from the neighbours, the coordinator contacted me to suggest I move to the tiny bedroom downstairs. It was further away from the nest in the attic and, coincidentally, most of the house's windows. I called another pest control company, this one province-wide with toll-free numbers, where I reached a woman named Jess.

"I'm currently living in a house with bat bugs. Would it be okay if I asked you a couple of questions?"

"Sure," she replied, but only seconds into the call, I could already tell she wasn't really paying attention.

"There's a bedroom downstairs, what if I move to it? Will I be visited less by the bugs. It's quite far away from their nest."

"They'll just follow you," Jess scoffed, as if she couldn't believe I'd be so stupid.

"You're sure?"

"Yeah," she said, the "h" coming in breathy and Valley-Girl-like. Then she snapped her gum in my ear.

I hung up wishing I'd called the woman in Swift Current instead. If I had, she would have lied to me, and that's what I'd really wanted.

I moved downstairs anyway. Not long after, I spotted a bug scampering across the kitchen floor. The coordinator told me to call whenever I saw live bugs, so I did. I'd thought of the first floor of the house as my safe space, and as I dialed her number, that little bit of make-believe dissolved. What she said next raised the little white hairs on my exposed ass.

"My husband says there's a hole in the chimney of the house. It's likely the bugs have invaded the basement too and are also coming up from below."

This was the exact moment I started to pack.

Terrified I would take the bugs home with me, I flitted back and forth to the house in a flesh-coloured towel, fresh from the dryer. The back of my makeshift garment billowed in the wind like a gown in a drafty hospital. I didn't see the couple walking briskly down the street until they were almost right in front of me. They stared, agog, as I shuffled something into the back seat and mooned them. The temperature was around zero, and my bare shoulders stung with lightly falling snowflakes.

"There's a bit of a bug problem with the house," I told them nervously, and they laughed as if I'd just told them the funniest joke they'd ever heard.

The drive home was a seven-hour stretch through rattlesnake country on single-lane highways. It didn't feel like I was going home, as much as it did like I was going backwards in time. As if, at the end of these seven hundred kilometres, the last eleven days would not have happened. I would never have baked books and cold-called strangers and paraded naked through the streets of a strange town. But even as familiar sights spooled past—the wind-bent trees, the gophers, and geese—I knew this thought to be untrue. I knew because of the itch that persisted, a hot spiking presence, running like insect legs over my skin.

Wide Apart

Following a running injury to my right knee, I avoided my doctor until I could no longer ignore the pain. When I did make it to her office, she took one look at the steep rise of my kneecaps and commented, "You have very high patellas."

"Thank you?" I replied, not knowing what a patella was.

"It's not a compliment," she responded sternly. "It means you're more prone to injury. You need to see a physiotherapist. I think sports physio might be best."

"I'm not very sporty," I joked.

"Didn't you say you sustained this injury while running?"

"If you saw me doing it, I don't think you'd call it running."

She gave me a referral for physiotherapy, and a prescription for some pain meds, and I promised to come back in three months for a follow-up. Though we both knew I wouldn't.

I found a physiotherapist accepting new clients, although the clinic's set-up of cubicles separated by what looked to be shower curtains made me somewhat nervous. At my first appointment, I trailed behind a nurse who stopped at each curtain to listen.

"This one's free," she said at last, and flung open the curtain to reveal a surprised-looking woman sitting in her underwear, picking at her toes.

Further down the hallway, I settled into my own empty stall to wait. I could hear the doctor getting closer, because the *shhk* noise of curtains thrust open and the gasp of surprise that followed that sound grew louder every ten minutes or so.

When it was my turn, the physiotherapist started off by bending my knee-joint every which way. He even pressed a warm ear to the area—as if it were a seashell—and listened to the grinding of the cartilage.

"Well," he declared, a little too brightly, "it'll never be the same again." He then twisted the knee in a direction it did not normally go and asked, "Does this hurt?"

"What do you think?" I winced.

The appointment dragged on, the physiotherapist leaving me to dangle off the too-short table for long stretches of time. I'd brought along a collection of Barbara Gowdy's short stories, and he darted in right after I'd finished the one about the baby that gets killed by a ceiling fan.

"Good book?" he asked as I replaced my bookmark.

"The best."

He carried a machine that sent shocks into the tender meat under my kneecap. "Can you feel that?" he asked, as my leg jumped around on the table like a fish pulled out of water.

"Yes," I gasped.

"I'll turn it up a bit then," he said, as if he hadn't heard. He cranked the dial, and I watched as my leg began to perform its own stunts, independent of the rest of my body. I had to grip the table to keep from launching off it. "I'll be back in about fifteen minutes," he promised. "While I'm gone, don't touch the machine."

After he dove through the curtain once more, I turned the machine down until the white spots blooming across my vision ceased to replicate. When he returned, it was with lettuce in his teeth. He shut off the machine, and my leg continued to spasm for several minutes.

"No running," he forbade, "at least not for some time yet. In the meantime, I recommend swimming laps."

While I healed, I was to do several exercises and ice the area twice a day. The latter became a high point. I'd ice the joint before bed and then place the frigid area on my partner's warm, bare skin. The jolt of cold made him squirm away from me, relinquishing his hold on the blankets.

I took to visiting the nearest pool in the afternoons, when it was only me, the new moms and their squalling children, and hordes of elderly people. This last group seemed to never get in the pool at all but were content to sit completely nude in the changing room, their legs wide-open, fanning their vaginas. I would change, swim, and return to the room an hour later to find that the original women hadn't moved at all—though they had somehow managed to multiply. Now they took up all the available benches, so I had to balance on one slick flip-flop as I wrestled my damp skin into a pair of jeans.

While the women seemed content to loaf in the too-humid changeroom, eating Tupperware containers of grapes and fawning over the infants that came through, the men actually made it to the pool. They swam with strokes that took up entire lanes and wore ancient, threadbare swim trunks, their pendulous genitals captured in a sort of gossamer that floated perilously close to my face.

Still, I kept going. After a few weeks, I'd gotten past the point of finding myself stuck in my car, my right leg frozen, as I rolled out into the snowy driveway and fought to get the limb to bend. The front crawl was comfortable, though the twisting motion of the breast-stroke kick seemed a long way off. I increased the number of laps every time I went and always sat in the hot tub afterwards, steeping the joint and trying to pretend that the woman next to me wasn't obviously masturbating with the jets.

Despite my reservations, I returned to the same physiotherapist. It was clear we had both decided that, given the briefness of our interaction (three appointments paid by Alberta Health Services), we were not going to bother to learn each other's names.

"How's the knee, ma'am?" he asked.

"Oh, I'm sure you know, Doc," I replied. "Not as bad as last week but still not great."

He took me through a series of new exercises, most of which required equipment I had never seen before: weights with several straps and boards with dozens of round protrusions I had to balance on.

"Where do I purchase these things so I can use them at home?" I wanted to know.

"You don't really need them," he assured me, placing a ball under my knee and looping what might've been an old sock filled with nickels over my extended foot.

"Then why teach me the exercises with them?"

"What?"

"Nothing."

He cranked his torture machine higher than ever and sprinted off, I imagined, to make bets with his assistants on how long I could stand it. While I watched the limb flail, I thought about my life before the injury.

Running is a solo sport. I live in a suburb that's barely within city limits. Except for the occasional coyote, I mostly had the nearby trails to myself. But in the pool, I had company.

I thought of the man who was convinced he was faster than everyone else. "You're not going to be one of those assholes that do breaststroke in the fast lane, are you?" he asked me once. And I, in response, somehow managed to swallow a mouthful of water. There was also the woman who insisted on swimming in the middle of the lane, causing me to flip onto my side when she sped past. The water would rush over my sudden stillness, as if I had stood too close to a train while wearing only my underwear.

Yet there were high points too, like the synchronized swimmer who turned in tight, graceful circles when we shared a lane. Even if her feet did sometimes skim my face and had once caught in the stretched-out bottom of my bathing suit. She'd been so pleasantly contrite when unwinding her toes from my garment.

When I passed the women headed up to the stationary bikes on the pool mezzanine, some of them in full makeup, I felt almost as if I were in disguise. I wore my swim cap squashed down low on my skull, and my goggles so tight that they left deep rings around my eyes for a long time after I'd left the pool. The first time my boyfriend saw the one-piece that I wore the most often, he recoiled, "What the hell is that? It's hideous."

"I like it."

"When did you even buy it?"

"While out shopping with your mother."

The physiotherapist returned to interrupt my reverie. He removed the adhesive paddles and asked how I was feeling.

"Like there's a hive of bees living under my skin," I told him.

"Oh you," he chided. "See you next week?"

"I suppose so," I called out, for he was already disappearing between the gap in the curtains. When he was gone, I tried to stand and crumpled to the floor.

Somewhere in my poolside journey, the old women in the change room sparked something in me. I envied the way they sprawled, dipping into a shared box of doughnuts, not bothering to brush the crumbs from their hands before smoothing each other's hair into rollers.

I tried to mirror their nonchalance as I pulled off my bra and felt the draft from the air vent above my nipples. One of the women paused, mid-bite, her gaze landing on my stretchmarks. I felt the hot flare of embarrassment singe the skin of my bare chest, as I threw my backpack over one shoulder and darted into a changing stall.

I saw my physiotherapist just once more after that. He called me by my first name, and I took this as a sort of parting gift from a man I would forever associate with small electric shocks.

"Lay back and try to relax," he instructed.

I did so as he yanked my legs in various directions like I was some sort of vulgar ornament. As I had a hundred times before, I wondered again whether this was part of the examination or if he was just screwing around. While he contorted my left leg around his waist, he advised, "You can always come back you know. But only if you want to."

"I don't mean to be rude," I ventured carefully, not wanting to set him off and be subjected to more time with his beloved machine, "but why would I want to come back?"

"I mean, like, if the knee really starts bothering you again, or if you injure yourself further. You can probably start running in a month though. You'll know when you're ready."

"Will I know this before or after I've ruined all of our work?"

"Probably after," he replied cheerfully.

He left me in the room, rocking on a beveled piece of wood. He'd given me no instructions of how many repetitions I was supposed to complete. A nurse discovered me some time later.

"You'll have to clear out," she hustled me. "We have other patients that need the room."

I still haven't returned to running. Every now and then I walk the trails near my house, pausing to pet the dogs that come through. They're all so much calmer now that I'm not sprinting past. On these walks I fantasize about breaking into a run, but I know the joint isn't ready.

Instead, I return to the pool, where those old women seem to have never left. They're laying down now, sprawling across the painted wooden benches as if impersonating the subjects of Grecian paintings. I, meanwhile, have given up on the closed-in single changerooms. I strip down in the main room now and, when I do, I can feel it coming on. That day when I never go beyond the change room, when I settle into a spot between two of the women and say, “That looks like a nice place to sit for a while. Shove over.” My knees springing wide apart.

Acknowledgements

Thank you to all who helped with the writing of this collection. To Jannie Edwards, who saw something in me all those years ago and worked on these essays with me for the last decade. To all who gave me advice about the process of putting together a book, most notably Daniel Scott Tysdal, Michael Hingston, and Astrid Blodgett.

Thank you to the journals where earlier incarnations of some of these essays were first published. "Reasons to Live" appeared in *Swamp Pink*, "Wide Apart" in *Room Magazine*, and "Important Intersection Ahead" in *The Fiddlehead.*

Thank you to my other mothers, Cindy Aubin and Cheryl Caul, who helped me along the way. Thank you Nick Purger for feeding me and always being an excellent sounding board—things are never quite so clear as they are after an evening spent in your company.

Thank you to the friends who let me use their stories in this book, especially Diane Allison and Carline Lemire. Thank you as well to St. Peter's Abbey for giving me space to write and to Father Demetrius for your counsel. Thank you to Lee and Dianne at Austin Bat Refuge for teaching me even more about bats (and letting me pet one!). They are more than worthy of your donations.

Thank you to my editor, Jennifer Bowering Delisle, for seeing my vision with this project and helping me carry it through.

Thank you to my family, without your influence I wouldn't have become a writer. Take that how you like. Thank you to my brother Gabe, for doing his best to protect me and for coming to get me when I called.

And thank you to Jack, for teaching me how to fight for the things that matter most.

Danica Klewchuk lives in Edmonton, Alberta. Her work has been published in a number of journals including *Event*, *Swamp Pink*, *On Spec*, and *Room*. *Standing in the Footprints of Beasts* is her first book.